I0794321

Principles in Practice

The Principles in Practice imprint offers teachers concrete illustrations of effective classroom practices based in NCTE research briefs and policy statements. Each book discusses the research on a specific topic, links the research to an NCTE brief or policy statement, and then demonstrates how those principles come alive in practice: by showcasing actual classroom practices that demonstrate the policies in action; by talking about research in practical, teacher-friendly language; and by offering teachers possibilities for rethinking their own practices in light of the ideas presented in the books. Books within the imprint are grouped in strands, each strand focused on a significant topic of interest.

Adolescent Literacy Strand

Adolescent Literacy at Risk? The Impact of Standards (2009) Rebecca Bowers Sipe
Adolescents and Digital Literacies: Learning Alongside Our Students (2010) Sara Kajder
Adolescent Literacy and the Teaching of Reading: Lessons for Teachers of Literature (2010) Deborah Appleman
Rethinking the "Adolescent" in Adolescent Literacy (2017) Sophia Tatiana Sarigianides, Robert Petrone, and Mark A. Lewis
Restorative Justice in the English Language Arts Classroom (2019) Maisha T. Winn, Hannah Graham, and Rita Renjitham Alfred

Writing in Today's Classrooms Strand

Writing in the Dialogical Classroom: Students and Teachers Responding to the Texts of Their Lives (2011) Bob Fecho
Becoming Writers in the Elementary Classroom: Visions and Decisions (2011) Katie Van Sluys
Writing Instruction in the Culturally Relevant Classroom (2011) Maisha T. Winn and Latrise P. Johnson
Writing Can Change Everything: Middle Level Kids Writing Themselves into the World (2020) Shelbie Witte, editor
Growing Writers: Principles for High School Writers and Their Teachers (2021) Anne Elrod Whitney

Literacy Assessment Strand

Our Better Judgment: Teacher Leadership for Writing Assessment (2012) Chris W. Gallagher and Eric D. Turley
Beyond Standardized Truth: Improving Teaching and Learning through Inquiry-Based Reading Assessment (2012) Scott Filkins
Reading Assessment: Artful Teachers, Successful Students (2013) Diane Stephens, editor
Going Public with Assessment: A Community Practice Approach (2018) Kathryn Mitchell Pierce and Rosario Ordoñez-Jasis

Literacies of the Disciplines Strand

Entering the Conversations: Practicing Literacy in the Disciplines (2014) Patricia Lambert Stock, Trace Schillinger, and Andrew Stock
Real-World Literacies: Disciplinary Teaching in the High School Classroom (2014) Heather Lattimer
Doing and Making Authentic Literacies (2014) Linda Denstaedt, Laura Jane Roop, and Stephen Best

Reading in Today's Classrooms Strand

Connected Reading: Teaching Adolescent Readers in a Digital World (2015) Kristen Hawley Turner and Troy Hicks

Digital Reading: What's Essential in Grades 3–8 (2015) William L. Bass II and Franki Sibberson

Teaching Reading with YA Literature: Complex Texts, Complex Lives (2016) Jennifer Buehler

Teaching English Language Learners Strand

Beyond "Teaching to the Test": Rethinking Accountability and Assessment for English Language Learners (2017) Betsy Gilliland and Shannon Pella

Community Literacies en Confianza: *Learning from Bilingual After-School Programs* (2017) Steven Alvarez

Understanding Language: Supporting ELL Students in Responsive ELA Classrooms (2017) Melinda J. McBee Orzulak

Writing across Culture and Language: Inclusive Strategies for Working with ELL Writers in the ELA Classroom (2017) Christina Ortmeier-Hooper

Students' Rights to Read and Write Strand

Adventurous Thinking: Fostering Students' Rights to Read and Write in Secondary ELA Classrooms (2019) Mollie V. Blackburn, editor

In the Pursuit of Justice: Students' Rights to Read and Write in Elementary School (2020) Mariana Souto-Manning, editor

Already Readers and Writers: Honoring Students' Rights to Read and Write in the Middle Grade Classroom (2020) Jennifer Ochoa, editor

Children's and YA Literature Strand

Challenging Traditional Classroom Spaces with YA Literature: Students in Community as Course Co-Designers (2022) Ricki Ginsberg

Restorying Young Adult Literature: Expanding Students' Perspectives with Digital Texts (2023) James Joshua Coleman, Autumn A. Griffin, and Ebony Elizabeth Thomas

Technology in the Classroom Strand

Reimagining Literacies in the Digital Age: Multimodal Strategies to Teach with Technology (2022) Pauline S. Schmidt and Matthew J. Kruger-Ross

Literacies Before Technologies: Making Digital Tools Matter for Middle Grades Learners (2023) Troy Hicks and Jill Runstrom

Restorying Young Adult Literature

Expanding Students' Perspectives with Digital Texts

James Joshua Coleman
University of Iowa

Autumn A. Griffin
Georgia State University

Ebony Elizabeth Thomas
University of Michigan

NCTE National Council of Teachers of English

340 N. Neil St., Suite #104, Champaign, Illinois 61820
www.ncte.org

Staff Editor: Cynthia Gomez
Imprint Editor: Cathy Fleischer
Interior Design: Victoria Pohlmann
Cover Design: Pat Mayer
Cover Images: NCTE/Marvin Young and iStock.com/DMEPhotography

ISBN 978-0-8141-0124-7 (paperback); 978-0-8141-0125-4 (epub); 978-0-8141-0127-8 (PDF)

Library of Congress Control Number: 2023934387

Dedication

We dedicate this book to restory-ers past and present.

To those young people who, even when erased and unimagined, have written themselves into existence.

Dear Reader,

As a former high school teacher, I remember the frustration I felt when the gap between Research (and that is how I always thought of it: Research with a capital R) and my own practice seemed too wide to ever cross. So many research studies were easy to ignore, in part because they were so distant from my practice and in part because I had no one to help me see how that research would make sense in my everyday practice.

That gap informs the thinking behind this book imprint. Designed for busy teachers, Principles in Practice publishes books that look carefully at NCTE's research reports and policy statements and puts those policies to the test in actual classrooms. The goal: to familiarize teachers with important teaching issues, the research behind those issues, and potential resources, and—most of all—make the research and policies come alive for teacher-readers.

This book is part of the strand that focuses on Children's and YA Literature. Each book in this strand highlights a different way to think about this topic—whether you're a classroom teacher or an English educator—and is organized in a similar way: immersing you first in the research principles surrounding teaching children's and YA literature (as laid out in the NCTE position statement *Preparing Teachers with Knowledge of Children's and Young Adult Literature*) and then taking you into actual classrooms to see how the principles play out. Each book closes with a teacher-friendly annotated bibliography to offer you even more resources.

Good teaching is connected to strong research. We hope these books help you continue the good teaching that you're doing, think hard about ways to adapt and adjust your practice, and grow even stronger and more confident in the vital work you do with kids every day.

Best of luck,

Cathy Fleischer
Imprint Editor

Contents

Acknowledgments

We would like to thank the National Council of Teachers of English (NCTE) for welcoming this book project and for supporting us through each iteration of *Restorying Young Adult Literature*. In particular, Cathy Fleischer's unflagging editorial eye allowed this book to take shape, and we would like to express our gratitude to her: Thank you, Cathy, sincerely. We would also like to thank all the staff who supported the production of this book project, from responding to emails to generating consent forms to typesetting. Although we do not know all the hands who have touched this book, we thank you.

We would also like to extend thanks to the University of Pennsylvania's Reading/Writing/Literacy (RWL) program, which brought the three of us (and so many of our contributing authors) together. The ethos and unwavering critical perspective that orients this book was cultivated in that space, and for that, we are thankful. Without RWL, this book would not exist.

Josh would also like to express his gratitude to Ebony and Autumn for their constant intellectual and emotional support throughout the writing of this book. Working with each of you was not merely an opportunity to weave together our words, our worlds, and our hearts; it was also a series of moments infused with laughter, love, and care that buoyed me through a global pandemic. Thank you both for making this project exactly what it was and exactly what I needed. I am so thankful and honored I was able to do this with you.

Autumn would like to thank Josh and Ebony for their love, genuine kindness, support, and thought partnership, as coauthors, colleagues, mentors, and friends. We would also like to extend our collective gratitude to our friends and family, those individuals whose constant support in our lives makes everything else—including this book—possible.

Ebony would like to thank Josh and Autumn for the gift of this book. As your mentor, I am forever proud of you both; as your friend, I am filled with gratitude and so much hope. I am thankful for both of you, as well as our contributors, the Super Friends research team, the Penn GSE comms team who worked on our annual Best Books lists, and our Philadelphia Writing Project and Reading/Writing/Literacy families.

Finally, we want to thank our readers. We believe you are the future of English language arts and, more important, the world. Thank you for taking the time to engage with our thoughts, our strategies, and our dreams. We hope this book will support you in developing your pedagogical approaches that realize social change in your classrooms. Finally, we hope this book will advance the study of young adult literature to help realize equity and justice in today's digital age.

Preparing Teachers with Knowledge of Children's and Young Adult Literature

This statement, formerly known as **Preparing Teachers with Knowledge of Children's and Adolescent Literature,** *was updated in July 2018 with the new title,* **Preparing Teachers with Knowledge of Children's and Young Adult Literature.**

Originally created by NCTE Children's Literature Assembly (CLA), 2004, revised July 2018

OVERVIEW

Purpose: Given increased calls for diversity in the English language arts curriculum and growing awareness of the need for young people to see themselves in the books they read, NCTE has commissioned an updated statement on preparing teachers with knowledge of children's and young adult literature.

Key Message: Research shows that when students are given the chance to read books that respect the questions, challenges, and emotions of childhood and adolescence, they read with greater interest and investment (Buehler, 2016; Mueller, 2001). Research also shows that teachers who are readers themselves do a better job of engaging their students in reading (Morrison, Jacobs, & Swinyard, 1999). Thus, teacher educators must support preservice teachers as they build rich and deep knowledge of children's and young adult literature over the course of their certification programs. Then teachers must invest in their own continued growth, learning, and development as children's and young adult literature advocates throughout their professional lives.

Context: A committee of English educators has updated NCTE's 2004 statement *Preparing Teachers with Knowledge of Children's and Adolescent Literature* by calling teachers at all stages of their careers to cultivate knowledge of books for young people, be readers of these books themselves, affirm diversity in book selection, and teach children's and young adult literature in ways that honor the books' literary quality as well as their potential to spark personal and social transformation.

STATEMENT

Evidence indicates that teachers' knowledge of children's and young adult literature is inconsistent and uneven from community to community, school to school, and classroom to classroom. Preservice teachers do not read any more than the general population (McKool & Gespass, 2009). Many of today's teachers have never taken a class in children's and young adult literature, and some states have eliminated the requirement for a dedicated course in children's and/or young adult literature for teaching certification. A growing number of schools no longer employ a librarian, who may be the only professional in the building who has formal training in children's and young adult literature, collection development, and matching young readers with books. Without librarians, the burden for reading advisory and material selection falls to classroom teachers, who often lack the training needed to perform these tasks.

Therefore, teacher education programs have the opportunity—and the responsibility—to

- *introduce* preservice teachers to books for children and teens;
- *develop* preservice teachers' understanding of the inherent value of these books for both general reading and classroom use;
- *raise* preservice teachers' awareness of the power of these books to affirm lived experience, create empathy, catalyze conversations, and respect the questions, challenges, and emotions of childhood and adolescence;
- *call* preservice teachers to embrace the roles of reading advocate and book matchmaker alongside their work as implementers of curriculum;
- *inspire* preservice teachers to commit to reading these books throughout their professional lives;
- *cultivate* in preservice teachers a commitment to teaching these books in ways that honor their literary quality as well as their potential to spark personal and social transformation;
- *build* preservice teachers' capacity for continued growth, learning, and development as advocates of children's and young adult literature.

As an organization, NCTE compels teachers at all stages of their careers to invest in books for young people—as readers of those books and as advocates for their worth in the classroom.

Recommendations

NCTE recommends that teacher educators and teachers commit to the following four principles in the service of increasing their ability to teach and advocate for children's and young adult literature.

1. **Know the literature.**

   Preservice teachers should cultivate book knowledge throughout various methods courses and across their entire teacher preparation program, regardless of state certification requirements. They should develop broad and sustained knowledge of quality books in the fields of children's and young adult literature, including fiction, nonfiction, and multimodal texts.

   At the same time, they should build knowledge of resources—including review journals, websites and blogs, social media discussions, book awards, and author appearances at local libraries and bookstores—that can provide them with information about quality new books and their potential for classroom use and reading advisory.

   They should also invest in relationships with librarians and organizations such as NCTE and ALAN (Assembly on Literature for Adolescents of NCTE) that can help them build capacity to discuss and recommend books, evaluate literature, remain current, and discover new ways to teach children's and young adult literature effectively.

2. **Be readers.**

   Teachers who are engaged readers do a better job of engaging students as readers. According to Morrison, Jacobs, and Swinyard (1999), "perhaps the most influential teacher behavior to influence students' literacy development is personal reading, both in and out of school" (p. 81). Teachers should commit to leading literate lives and becoming connected to reading communities—whether in person or through social media—that support them as readers and literacy professionals. Teachers should understand the value of different modes and platforms for reading (Garcia & O'Donnell-Allen, 2015) and build their capacity to read with a critical, discerning eye (Newkirk, 2011).

3. **Affirm diversity and exercise critical literacy.**

   In alignment with NCTE's Resolution on the Need for Diverse Children's and Young Adult Books (2015), NCTE challenges teachers and teacher educators to assume a transformative activist stance (Stetsenko, 2016) that supports a future of equality for all youth by engaging students with diverse books, which offer readers what scholar Rudine Sims Bishop (1990) calls windows, mirrors, and sliding glass doors. It is essential that youth have access to books in which they can see themselves and engage with the lives of others (see, for example, platforms created by the current and former National Ambassadors for Young People's Literature, including Jacqueline Woodson, Gene Luen Yang, and Walter Dean Myers). NCTE believes that books help readers transform their lives and expand their visions of the world.

   Nevertheless, there is a dearth of diverse books for youth in the United States as seen in yearly statistics about trends in multicultural children's book publishing prepared by the Cooperative Children's Book Center (CCBC) of the School of Education at the University of Wisconsin-Madison. The #WeNeedDiverseBooks and #ReadInColor social media campaigns have illuminated the paucity of diverse books in the marketplace. Although the CCBC recently observed that children's picture books feature an increased number of characters with "brown skin . . . of unspecified race or ethnicity, with no visible culturally specific markers in either the story or the art," the CCBC questions whether books with racially ambiguous characters provide actual windows, mirrors, and sliding doors for today's readers (Horning, Lindgren, Schliesman, & Tyner, 2018, n.p.). NCTE joins the CCBC in urging educators to not only advocate for more authentically diverse children's and young adult books from US publishers, but also to support authors, illustrators, publishers, and booksellers whose work represents multiple perspectives and cultural diversity in the lives of all children.

   In addition to being advocates and supporters of diverse literature for youth, educators who assume a transformative activist stance must build their capacities for discernment and critical evaluation so they are prepared to choose children's and YA books wisely and strategically from the books available to them. Simply because a book features diverse characters does not mean that the book endorses equality and/or cultural understanding (Apol, Sakuma, Reynolds, & Rop, 2003; Dávila, 2012). For example, some popular works of contemporary, "multicultural" realistic fiction privilege the assumption that all residents of the United States should embrace dominant mainstream culture (e.g., *My Name is Yoon* [Recorvitis, 2003]; *One Green Apple* [Bunting, 2006]). Some of these books reinforce assimilation social narratives (Yoon, Simpson, & Haag, 2010) and/or endorse monocultural language and identity (Ghiso & Campano, 2013). Educators and students should collectively cultivate critical literacy practices to critique the social narratives that are endorsed by the books they select (Leland, Lewison, & Harste, 2012; Morrell, 2007) and talk back to the literature (Enciso, 1997).

   Educators who affirm diversity and exercise critical literacy as part of a transformative activist stance recognize that they are always learning and expanding their capacities for transformation. They are open to guiding difficult discussions about inequality with students and are willing to tolerate the possibilities of "wobbling" while they explore uncharted territories with students (e.g., Fecho, 2005; Garcia & O'Donnell-Allen, 2015). They recognize that children's books are political (Nodelman, 2008; Stephens, 1992) and are the artifacts of the authors', illustrators', and/or publishers' views of the world (Willis & Harris, 2003) and/or US history (Thomas, Reese, & Horning, 2016). Moreover, these educators follow national conversations via media and blogs about diverse books, especially related to issues of power and representation (e.g., Reading While White; American Indians in Children's Books).

4. **Use appropriate pedagogy.**

   Teaching children's and young adult literature is about more than getting students to fall in love with reading. Preservice teachers also need to learn appropriate and effective strategies for helping students find books that will engage them as readers and as participants in critical, significant conversations about their lives (NCTE, 2006; Tschida, Ryan, & Ticknor, 2014). This requires a deep knowledge of excellent books and the willingness to carefully curate a classroom library that provides appropriate choices for all students (Crisp, Knezek, Quinn, Bingham, Girardeau, & Starks, 2016; NCTE, 2017). Preservice teachers also need to know evidence-based strategies for supporting student knowledge of literary crafting—that is, how authors develop characters, construct plots, and employ other literary elements to create an exemplary work. Examining literary craft does not mean that the focus is on dissecting a book's structure or meaning. Rather, teachers should be skilled at helping students develop a common language for determining what makes a book excellent literature. Finally, teachers need to know how to advocate for the freedom and autonomy to create classrooms that support research-based pedagogical strategies for teaching children's and young adult literature (Mathis et al., 2014; NCTE Children's Literature Assembly, 2004).

WORKS CITED

Apol, L., Sakuma, A., Reynolds, T. M., & Rop, S. K. (2003). "When can we make paper cranes?" Examining pre-service teachers' resistance to critical readings of historical fiction. *Journal of Literacy Research, 34,* 429–464.

Buehler, J. (2016). *Teaching reading with YA literature: Complex texts, complex lives.* Urbana, IL: NCTE.

Bunting, E. (2006). *One green apple.* New York, NY: Houghton Mifflin.

Crisp, T., Knezek, S. M., Quinn, M., Bingham, G., Girardeau, K., and Starks, F. (2016). "What's on our bookshelves? The diversity of children's literature in early childhood classroom libraries." *Journal of Children's Literature 42*(2), 29–42.

Dávila, D. (2012). In search of the ideal reader for children's non-fiction books about el Día de Los Muertos. *Journal of Children's Literature, 38*(1), 16–26.

Enciso, P. (1997). Negotiating the meaning of difference: Talking back to multicultural literature. In T. Rogers & A. Soter (Eds.), *Reading across cultures* (pp. 13–41). New York, NY: Teachers College Press.

Fecho, B. (2001). "Why are you doing this?" Acknowledging and transcending threat in a critical inquiry classroom. *Research in the Teaching of English, 36*(1), 9–37.

Garcia, A., & O'Donnell-Allen, C. (2015). *Pose, wobble, flow: A culturally proactive approach to literacy instruction.* New York, NY: Teachers College Press.

Ghiso, M., & Campano, G. (2013). Ideologies of language and identity in U.S. children's literature. *Bookbird, 51*(3), 47–55.

Horning, K., Lindgren, M., Schliesman, M., & Tyner, M. (2018). A few observations: Literature in 2017. *CCBC Choices 2018*. Madison, WI: Cooperative Children's Book Center. Retrieved from: http://ccbc.education.wisc.edu/books/choiceintro18.asp[1]

Leland, C., Lewison, M., & Harste, J. (2012). *Teaching children's literature: It's critical.* New York, NY: Routledge.

Mathis, J. B., Aziz, S., Crisp, T., Graff, J. M., Kesler, T., Liang, L. A., Sekeres, D. C., & Wilfong, L. (2014). Teaching children's literature in the 21st century. *Journal of Children's Literature, 39*(1), 56–61.

McKool, S. S., & Gespass, S. (2009). Does Johnny's reading teacher love to read? How teachers' personal reading habits affect instructional practices. *Literacy Research and Instruction,48*(3), 264–276.

Morrell, E. (2007). *Critical literacy and urban youth: Pedagogies of access, dissent, and liberation.* New York, NY: Routledge.

Morrison, T. G., Jacobs, J. S., & Swinyard, W. R. (1999). Do teachers who read personally use recommended literacy practices in their classrooms? *Literacy Research and Instruction, 38*(2), 81–100.

Moss, B., & Young, T. A. (2010). *Creating lifelong readers through independent reading.* Newark, DE: International Reading Association.

Mueller, P. N. (2001). *Lifers: Learning from at-risk adolescents.* Portsmouth, NH: Heinemann.

National Council of Teachers of English. (2006). *Resolution on preparing and certifying teachers with knowledge of children's and adolescent literature.* Urbana, IL: NCTE.

National Council of Teachers of English. (2015). *Resolution on the need for diverse books.* Urbana, IL: NCTE.

National Council of Teachers of English. (2017). *Statement on classroom libraries.* Urbana, IL: NCTE.

NCTE Children's Literature Assembly. (2004). *Preparing teachers with knowledge of children's and adolescent literature.* Urbana, IL: NCTE.

Newkirk, T. (2011). *The art of slow reading: Six time-honored practices for engagement.* Portsmouth, NH: Heinemann.

Nodelman, P. (2008). *The hidden adult.* Baltimore: The Johns Hopkins University Press.

Recorvitis, H. (2003). *My name is Yoon.* New York, NY: Farrar, Straus and Giroux.

Sims Bishop, R. (1990). Mirrors, windows, and sliding glass doors. *Perspectives, 1*(3), ix–xi.

Stephens, J. (1992). *Language and ideology in children's fiction.* New York, NY: Longman.

Stetsenko, A. (2016). *The transformative mind: Expanding Vygotsky's approach to development and education.* New York, NY: Cambridge University Press.

Thomas, E., Reese, D., & Horning, K. (2016). Much ado about *A fine dessert*: The cultural politics of representing slavery in children's literature. *Journal of Children's Literature, 42*(2), 6–17.

Tschida, C., Ryan, C., & Ticknor, R. (2014). Building on windows and mirrors: Encouraging the disruption of "single stories" through children's literature. *Journal of Children's Literature, 40*(1), 28–39.

Willis, A., & Harris, V. (1997). Preparing preservice teachers to teach multicultural literature. In J. Flood, S. Brice Heath, & D. Lapp (Eds.), *Handbook of research on teaching literacy through the communicative and visual arts* (pp. 460–469). New York, NY: Macmillan Library Reference USA.

Yoon, B., Simpson, A., & Haag, C. (2010). Assimilation ideology: Critically examining underlying messages in multicultural literature. *Journal of Adolescent & Adult Literacy, 54*(2), 109–118.

STATEMENT AUTHORS

This document was revised by an NCTE working committee comprising the following:

Jennifer Buehler, Chair – Saint Louis University, St. Louis, MO

Denise Dávila – The University of Texas at Austin

Amy McClure – Ohio Wesleyan University, Delaware, OH

Donalyn Miller – Author and Consultant, Colleyville, TX

Introduction

Chapter One

The 2020s continue the current century's fascination with digital storytelling in all its myriad forms. From ebooks factoring into *New York Times* bestseller sales to prestige films and TV programs debuting on new streaming platforms, the role of the internet in narrative production, dissemination, and consumption cannot be overstated—and that was before COVID-19's profound impact on the world. With schools, the workplace, libraries, and even the entertainment industry moving away from the public sphere and into private homes, the very way we access young adult literature, media, and culture has changed dramatically. Stories for and about youth and young adults circulate through our news and social media feeds; they sound through our televisions; and they blare through our headsets. Youth literature has, in today's digital age, transformed into a ubiquitous feature of life, and young people are harnessing these narratives to powerful effect. Confronting historical violence that circulates online as well as the realities of witnessing that violence (Chouliaraki, 2015; Papailias, 2016), young people—particularly those who identify as Black, Indigenous, and/or people of Color (BIPOC), queer, trans, disabled, and/or among these intersections—are using young adult literature (YAL) to reimagine futures both on and offline that are defined not by oppression but by justice and love (Griffin & Turner, 2021; Love, 2019; Mirra & Garcia, 2020; Muñoz, 2009).

Youth and young adults' online participation in virtual communities anticipated this shift to the digital long before the imperatives of the present moment necessitated it in classrooms. Although past work has documented this shift in fan cultures (Thomas & Stornaiuolo, 2016; 2019) as well as in activism and civic participation (Stornaiuolo & Thomas, 2017; 2018), teacher education (Coleman, 2020), and students' online identity development (Griffin, 2021), less attention has been paid to the ways this digital age shift has influenced young adult literature and media itself. While YAL has traditionally referred to print-based prose novels and, furthermore, been aligned with a certain understanding of "literary merit" (Cart, 2016), we believe that in today's digital era, YAL itself has changed. Both the digitization of YAL and the emergence of networked, participatory cultures surrounding that literature invite renewed consideration of what counts as "good" literature for young people. For example, expanded modes within texts (e.g., visuals, interactive graphics, and sound), as well as a whole new range of textual forms such as digital stories, fanvids, and more, invite expanded considerations of what constitutes YAL today. Moreover, YAL now circulates online in unprecedented quantities and at unprecedented speeds, and from creators and consumers to publishers, disseminators, and influencers, young people have harnessed *digital YAL* and *digital YA culture* to advocate and create a more just representational landscape for YAL. Not only are today's tweens and teens engaged in the agentive work of identity assertion and self-redefinition, but also restorying in the digital age has changed the textuality of young adult literature forever.

Restorying has been conceptualized in the narrative analysis tradition in qualitative research as a method for researchers to break down the stories participants tell into their constituent parts—plot, characters, themes—and then synthesize them in new ways to make meaning of myriad experiences documenting the same phenomenon (cf. Connelly & Clandinin, 2006; Daiute & Lightfoot, 2004; Ollerenshaw & Cresswell, 2002). However, restorying can also characterize the complex ways contemporary young people are critically narrating the word and the world (Freire & Macedo, 2005): it describes a process and practice of analyzing their lived experiences, then synthesizing and recontextualizing a multiplicity of stories in order to form new narratives. In other words, as young adult readers imagine themselves into stories, they *reimagine the very stories themselves* (Thomas & Stornaiuolo, 2016).

As proposed by Thomas and Stornaiuolo (2016), restorying involves altering six elements of narrative through acts of reading, writing, and imagining, and in doing so, teachers and students can craft new, more just narratives in their classrooms. As the outer circle of Figure 1.1 illustrates, restorying addresses the following narrative elements: identity, place, mode, perspective, metanarrative, and time, and the inner circle provides methods of restorying those elements. For instance, if a student were to restory identity, they might engage in racebending or queerbending to explore how a narrative might change if the primary character were BIPOC, queer, or both.

FIGURE 1.1. Forms of restorying.

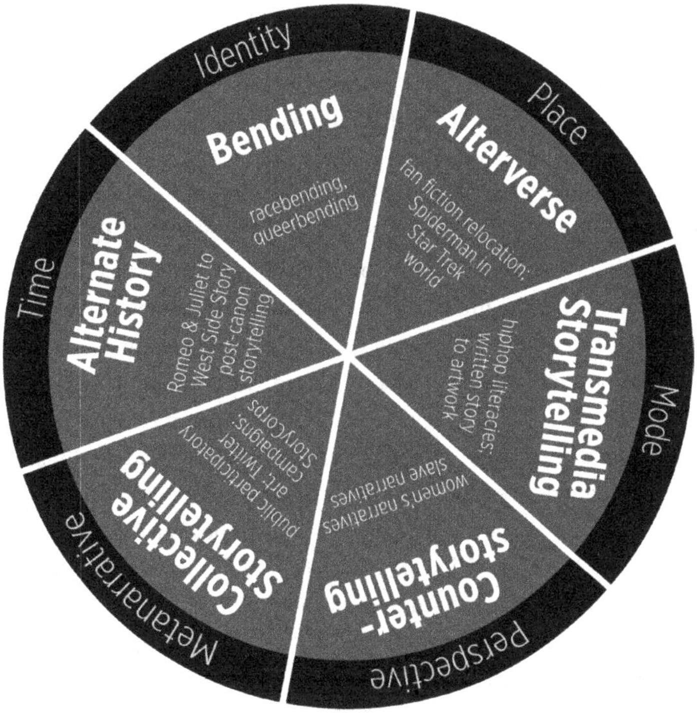

Throughout this book, we, the primary authors—Josh, Autumn, and Ebony—explore various aspects of restorying as it connects to teachers' and students' lives both in and beyond English language arts (ELA) contexts. Similarly, educators teaching young adult literature, media, and culture might ask students who are digitally engaged to imagine otherwise or to restory. Inviting students into the process of restorying has the potential to foster understanding about what remains essential about the human condition, even during our fractured, increasingly digital times. Just as important, ELA classrooms and their surrounding communities are the perfect location from which to restory the future.

Digital YAL and Digital YA Culture: Restoried Texts for Restoried Times

While restorying has wide-ranging potential, this volume's focus on pedagogical practice illuminates how two primary concepts (digital YAL and digital YA culture) might sit in contrast to traditional understandings of YAL and help us understand how restorying can influence ELA teaching and learning (see Table 1.1).

Traditionally, young adult literature has referred to a genre of literature for and about young adults, and these texts were generally print-based. (For more on the history of YAL, please see Cart's [2016] "Young Adult Literature: The State of a Restless Art.") Digital YAL, however, refers to shifting textual forms. In our digital era, YAL can no longer refer to print text alone, regardless of how beloved those print texts might be. The smell and feel of paper, while nostalgic for many of us teachers, does not characterize the totality of YAL any longer. Instead, digital YAL refers to literature for young adults that exists in all manner of digital forms and formats, and these, too, espouse literary quality. These might be a PDF on a Chromebook, ebooks housed on Kindles or phones, audiobooks blaring through headphones, and even .txt files published on fan community forums such as Wattpad. Such digital texts are restorying what it means to teach YAL, and they invite different forms of reading, participation, and meaning making. These texts provide instant translations and dictionary definitions, internet and audio experiences, inline commenting, and more, and all of these digital affordances invite young people to engage with YAL in new, critical ways. Embracing digital YAL provides teachers with expanded access to diverse textual forms and pedagogical approaches that invite students' stories and restories into their classrooms.

It's important to know that digital YAL does not exist in a vacuum but, instead, functions as part of a thriving online, participatory network of readers, authors, educators, and researchers. To spotlight the importance of this network for teaching and learning, we propose the term *digital YA culture*, which within the context of this book refers to blogs, social media feeds, fan communities, apps, and other digital platforms that allow YA enthusiasts to create social transformation through the circulation of, discussion of, and engagement with YAL and media. In short, twenty-first-century digital technologies are altering what it means to read, study, and teach YAL, and teachers can learn to harness these participatory cultures (Jenkins et al., 2016) to

TABLE 1.1. Book primary concepts.

Concepts	Definition
Young Adult Literature (YAL)	Refers to a genre of literature that focuses on the experiences of young adults. Traditionally, YAL has referred to print-based texts.
Digital YAL	Refers to literature for young adults that exists in all manner of digital forms and formats, and these, too, espouse literary quality.
Digital YA Culture	Refers to the network of blogs, social media feeds, fan communities, apps, and other digital platforms that allow YA enthusiasts to create social transformation through the circulation, discussion, and engagement with YAL and media.

galvanize antiracist, queer- and trans-affirming, and anti-ableist pedagogy. As described by Jenkins (2006), participatory cultures are characterized by

1. Relatively low barriers to artistic expression and civic engagement;
2. Strong support for creating and sharing one's creations with others;
3. Some type of informal mentorship whereby what is known by the most experienced is passed along to novices;
4. Spaces where members believe their contributions matter; and
5. Some degree of social connection among members feel some degree of social connection with one another (at least caring what other people think about what they have created).

For ELA teaching, attention to these five aspects of digital YA culture advances restorying efforts. It embraces the affordances of our digital era—both the quantity and the rapidity of shifts in YAL publishing and pedagogy—to center the knowledges, experiences, and histories of actual young adults. It tears down barriers to access and honors the reading and writing practices that young people already bring to the study of YAL and ELA.

For us, an embrace of digital YAL and digital YA culture is key in restorying a more just future for the teaching of English and for the world, and it aligns with this volume's guiding position statement. Entitled *Preparing Teachers with Knowledge of Children's and Young Adult Literature*, this NCTE statement provides four recommendations through which educators can realize those more just futures using children's and young adult literature. These are (1) know the literature, (2) be readers themselves, (3) affirm diversity and exercise critical literacy, and (4) use appropriate pedagogy. Interlocking, these recommendations address the shifting role that the reading and teaching of children's and young adult literature plays in twenty-first-century ELA instruction. As the position statement authors explain,

> A growing number of schools no longer employ a librarian, who may be the only professional in the building who has formal training in children's and young adult literature, collection development, and matching your readers with books. Without librarians, the burden for reading advisory and material selection falls to classroom teachers, who often lack the training needed to perform these tasks. (*Preparing Teachers*, 2018)

While we address librarianship specifically in Chapter 3, generally, the twenty-first century has shifted ELA teachers' responsibilities regarding text selection, access, curriculum development, and multimodality, specifically as it relates to children's and young adult literature. That reality is one this book seeks to address head-on.

Following the position statement, we believe the digital outlets (e.g., social media feeds, blogs, and various platforms) are playing an increasingly important role in shaping access and pedagogy to youth literature. Accordingly, in this book, we provide practical strategies for using children's and young adult literature to "spark personal and social transformation" (*Preparing Teachers*, 2018). Specifically, we use the position statement's four recommendations as a framework for exploring the following questions:

1. How can restorying traditional understandings of YAL help educators realize social justice in today's digital age?
2. How can pedagogy, advocacy, and activism through digital YAL and digital YA culture advance social justice in schools and communities?

This book seeks to expand the body of critical scholarship about YAL by spotlighting the ways in which adults and young people are restorying YAL online through digital tools. While focused on providing principles in practice for educators, throughout this book, we share the voices of students, teachers, librarians, and researchers, all of whom are harnessing digital YAL and digital YA culture to teach and restory more just social futures, both in and beyond the classroom.

Book Organization

Bringing together a symphony of experiences and expertise, this book has three primary authors, Josh, Autumn, and Ebony, who conceived, organized, and wrote *Restorying Young Adult Literature*. Throughout the book, "we" and "us" refer to our collective voice. However, specific sections of this book are cowritten by trusted colleagues, each of whom we invited based on their expertise and practitioner knowledges about teaching digital YAL. Introductions to each of our contributing authors can be located in the "Introducing the Authors and Our Approach" subsection below. Conceptually, the book is organized around restorying and core elements of ELA teaching, and each chapter illuminates a different pedagogical approach to teaching digital YAL and surrounding digital YA culture.

While in the first chapter we introduce the key background and major concepts guiding this book, Chapter 2, "Restorying Text Selection," dives into the heart of teaching and learning of digital YAL by focusing on text selection. Although historical publication gaps persist and BIPOC, queer, trans, and disabled folks remain underrepresented in YAL, the amount of digital YAL written by individuals of diverse, intersecting identities has skyrocketed. This reality, one characterized by simultaneous historical erasure and digital overabundance, can lead educators to experience a paradoxical feeling, one of both too little and an overabundance of diverse representation, which can stymie teachers' text selection. To address this feeling, the chapter explores the question: how do we address historical gaps in publishing while also navigating the perhaps overwhelming proliferation of diverse representation in digital YAL?

In response, Chapter 2 provides educators with a framework for restorying text selection and, per the position statement, coming to "know the literature." Drawing upon the core principles of the digital movement #Disrupt Texts, we demonstrate how one might disrupt historical trends in YAL publishing by (1) interrogating our own biases, (2) centering Black, Indigenous, and voices of color in literature, (3) applying a critical literacy lens to our teaching practices, and (4) working in the community with our antiracist educators. By reimagining text selection in light of these four principles, educators can navigate the paradoxical feeling of a simultaneous publishing gap and an overabundance of choices created by today's digital YAL and digital YA culture, and each principle is accompanied by a "Text Selection Reflection" section that provides guiding questions to aid teachers to cultivate restorying text selection practices. The chapter also provides a speculative literature unit written by contributing author Coyote Shook, a queer and trans educator, and it weaves together classic literature, YAL, and digital tools to aid students in navigating the speculation or reimagining of classroom teaching and learning.

Chapter 3, "Restorying Digital Access," extends efforts to restory YAL teaching and learning from the classroom into the library, and it specifically supports teachers in "be[ing] readers" and "us[ing] appropriate pedagogy" (*Preparing Teachers*, 2018). This chapter directly challenges deleterious narratives of the "digital divide." While certainly a valid concern for teaching digital YAL and culture today, the digital divide has been mobilized to position students as the haves and the have-nots, and often these perceptions of who has access and skills have fallen along racial lines. Confronting these narratives, contributing author Latrice Ferguson first details the state of librarianship relative to digital YAL today and then curates first-person accounts of current and former librarians to spotlight how teachers and librarians can work hand in hand to honor the funds of knowledge (Moll et al., 1992) students bring to learning with digital YAL. Specifically, she provides vignettes that demonstrate how librarians can support ELA educators as teacher-librarians, media specialists, reader advisors, and information literacy advocates; furthermore, she provides teachers with methods for inviting each form of librarian into your classrooms. Also in this chapter, we demonstrate how educators can #ReadWoke alongside their students. Started by award-winning librarian Cecily Lewis, the #ReadWoke campaign has circulated through digital YA culture to recommend YAL that can inform social justice–oriented teaching. In addition to the #ReadWoke initiative, we explore how Twitter feeds and blogs mobilize similar hashtags to promote access. Finally, this chapter includes three classroom connections teachers might immediately take up in their practices.

Disrupting literacy curricula as white property, Chapter 4 ("Restorying YAL Curricula") moves from a focus on actors and educators to a focus on the materials that make restorying YAL possible, particularly as it "affirm[s] diversity and exercise[s] critical literacy" (*Preparing Teachers*, 2018). We demonstrate how the historical roots of YAL and literacy curricula have tied the genre and its associated pedagogical practices to whiteness. To restory this reality, we detail a four-step process for cultivating a digital YAL curriculum and for using the racial literacy development pyramid (Price-Dennis & Sealey-Ruiz, 2021) to support teachers in recognizing and decentering whiteness in their YAL teaching. We then advocate turning to fandom as a tool through which teachers might un-whitewash their curriculum. From "Stopping the Stigma" to "Publishing Your Product," we provide an approachable strategy for using fandom to teach students restorying practices. Specifically, we detail identity bending (e.g., racebending, genderbending, speciesbending, etc.) as a compositional strategy through which students draw upon their lived experiences to write new stories into the world. This chapter then concludes by explaining how restorying with digital YA fandom provides one way to un-whitewash curricula.

Chapter 5, "Restorying Multimodality," rounds out our exploration of YA literature, culture, and composition, focusing on YA digital production on platforms and the "use [of] appropriate pedagogy" (*Preparing Teachers*, 2018). We present the production processes and compositions of two groups of youth alongside two English educators. Detailed by contributing author and doctoral student Bethany Monea, the first project is a YouTube page created by a group of Latina undergraduates, Perla Gonzalez, Joselyn Andrade, and Keiry Chicas, who, as contributing authors, explore their first year as college students during the pandemic; the second project, contributed by doctoral student Rabani Garg, is a series of digital artifacts created by a twelfth-grade student in India engaged in digital art activism. Putting these two projects into conversation, we conclude by arguing that inviting students to take the lead in their own learning and digital production places agency back in the hands of the students and allows for richer and more authentic learning experiences for students (Moll, 2019).

Finally, in Chapter 6, "Restorying the Future toward Hope," we imagine wildly to explore how teachers and students might use digital YAL and digital YA culture to build futures and hopescapes that center historically marginalized students within English language arts. Together, these chapters strive to provide both a critical orientation and a practical guide for integrating digital YAL and digital YA culture into English classrooms in the hope of restorying young adult literature and pedagogy for today's digital era.

Introducing the Authors and Our Approach

As we noted before, this book is authored by three primary authors and eight contributing authors. As the primary authors, Josh, Autumn, and Ebony came to know one another through shared research around diversity and YAL. James Joshua Coleman (he/they), or Josh as he is better known, earned his PhD in YAL studies while studying with Ebony Elizabeth Thomas (Ebony) (she/her) at the University of Pennsylvania. His scholarship spotlights the need for intersectional, queer, and trans representation in YAL, and he is currently an assistant professor of English education at the University of Iowa. After earning her doctorate from the University of Maryland, Autumn A. Griffin (she/her), or Autumn, worked with Ebony as a postdoctoral research Fellow at the University of Pennsylvania. Her work is currently focused on Black girlhoods, multimodal literacy, and diverse YAL. Further, Ebony Elizabeth Thomas (Ebony) has been internationally recognized for her scholarship in YAL. Her book *The Dark Fantastic* (2019) examines race and representation in contemporary YAL. Currently, she is co-chair and associate professor in the Joint Program of English and Education at the University of Michigan's School of Education.

The eight contributing authors represent friends, colleagues, and research partners of the three primary authors. Coyote Shook (they/them), for instance, who contributed the "Weird Science" section in Chapter 2, is a former high school ELA teacher who was an undergrad alongside Josh. They have remained friends for years and continue to share stories and research about their experiences as white queer educators. Latrice Ferguson (she/her), who wrote the section "Facilitating Digital Futures in the Classroom and Beyond" in Chapter 3, began her doctoral training under Ebony at the University of Pennsylvania and worked alongside both Josh and Autumn while there. Coauthor of the section "Engaging YouTube to Tell Our Stories" in Chapter 5, Bethany Monea (she/her) was also a student at the University of Pennsylvania, where she worked with all three of the primary authors. As part of her dissertation project, she worked with contributing undergraduate authors Perla Gonzalez (she/her), Joselyn Andrade (she/her), and Keiry Chicas (she/her) to disrupt dominant, white-centric narratives about college transitions on YouTube. Finally, Rabani Garg (she/her), who is also a doctoral student at the University of Pennsylvania, trained with Ebony and worked alongside Josh, Autumn, Latrice, and Bethany in various research capacities. As part of Rabani's internationally focused work on literacy and participatory communities, she introduced student author Shyamu Korwa (he/him) into this project to share his digital YA productions.

Together, Josh, Autumn, and Ebony planned and organized this book, and we worked alongside our contributing authors to ensure cohesion amongst sections and chapters. While each of us, the primary authors, has our own areas of expertise as well as lived experience, the book is a collective and collaborative effort to understand what restorying has been, is, and might yet be in ELA classrooms and beyond. *Restorying Young Adult Literature* brings together a symphony of perspectives, identities, and political commitments to consider the role of digital tools and technology in the teaching of young adult literature (YAL) today. Central to this text, intersectionality shapes both our organization of the book and who we included as contributing authors and in our citations. However, in writing the book, it became clear we could never represent the complete experiences and identities of the teachers and students we wrote both with and for. This led us to clarify our approach to writing this book and to name how intersectionality shaped our representation of various critical initiatives tied to YAL.

While seeking to include various intersections of identity, we can never represent the complexity of human identity, in its fullness. We have thus elected to represent the various critical commitments of our cowriters and those we cite as they name themselves. In essence, our naming of identity throughout this book aligns with authors' explicitly named identities in their work. We do this to represent individuals and their work on their own terms. However, it can create the impression, in moments, that certain individuals are not thinking intersectionally. For example, in our description of the four #DisruptTexts principles (see Chapters 2 and 4), these authors name an explicit commitment to centering BIPOC voices in the teaching of literature in ELA contexts. While queer, trans, disabled, citizenship status, and other identities are not named explicitly in these principles, we do not understand this work as incommensurate with a coalitional and intersectional politics across communities. Instead, we see this work as spotlighting a particular identity as a move toward equity and justice in ELA, and in fact, in broader writings, #DisruptTexts' intersectional commitments are made explicit.

Accordingly, for us, inclusion in this book was predicated on a clear and dedicated commitment to intersectional approaches in teaching and learning with young adult literature. So, while in moments, one or another community might be centered in ways that seem to forego an intersectional approach, we invite our readers to recognize this failing as a function of the limitations of writing and representation. We have done our best to spotlight moments of intersectional thinking for both our cowriters and the cited ELA educators; however, we invariably fail. We do, however, see the larger book as inviting a variety of intersectional perspectives that cover a wide gamut of human experience, and our hope is this book will animate a wide array of critical approaches that strive to challenge white supremacy, queerphobia and transphobia, ableism, misogyny, and more through embracing intersectional approaches to teaching YAL in today's digital world.

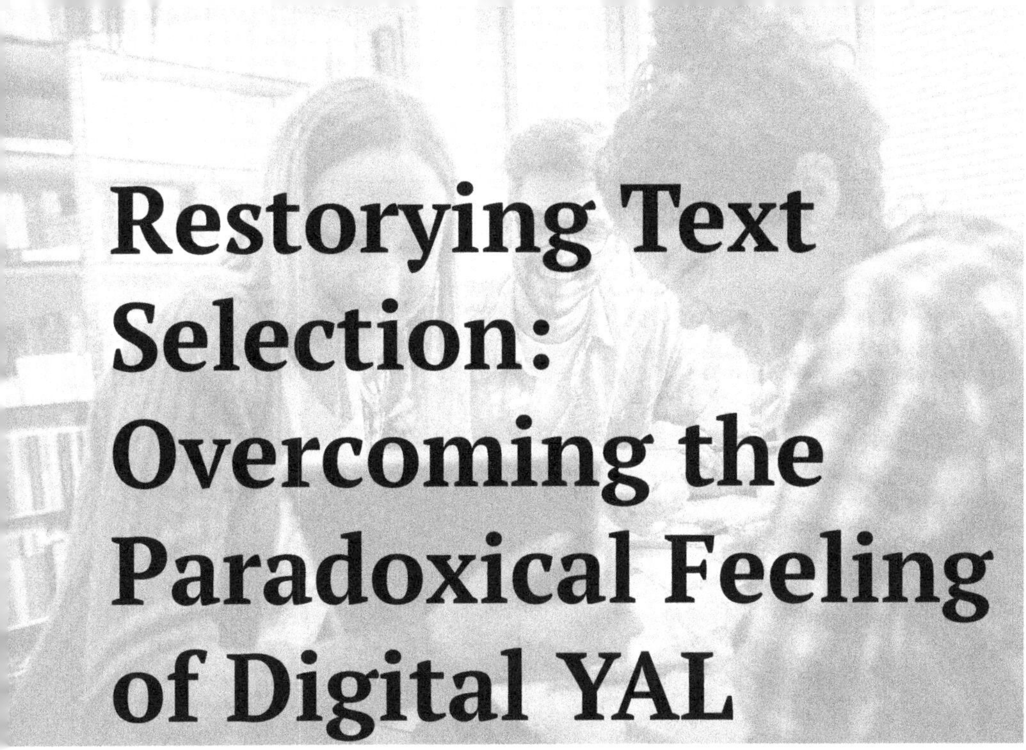

Chapter Two

Restorying Text Selection: Overcoming the Paradoxical Feeling of Digital YAL

Text selection remains one of the greatest challenges facing English teachers in the twenty-first century, and increased access to digital YAL and digital culture has amplified these concerns. Blogs, podcasts, and social media feeds are recommending young adult literature at unprecedented rates, and in a maelstrom of potential texts, how do teachers know which texts to select? For those of us concerned with issues of equity and justice, answers to this question center on representation, and Rudine Sims Bishop's (1990) iconic metaphors of "mirrors," "windows," and "sliding glass doors" have provided a litmus test for choosing multicultural literature for young people. Culturally responsive, these metaphors have been used to ensure students see themselves represented in literature (mirrors), have access to diverse representations (windows), and explore that diversity through imaginative acts of reading and writing (sliding glass doors). Reimagining representation has also provided a foothold for English teachers to address a central paradox generated by today's digital YA culture: the feeling of a simultaneous gap in and overabundance of digital YAL when selecting texts for our students and our classrooms.

This paradoxical feeling results from the contradictory and perhaps even overwhelming recognition that while substantial gaps in diverse representation in YAL persist historically, there is simultaneously a seeming overabundance of representations circulating right now in digital YA culture. Providing a historical snapshot, David Huyck and Sarah Park Dahlen's (2019) infographic (Figure 2.1) reveals representational gaps in twenty-first-century children's literature.

FIGURE 2.1. Diversity in children's books 2018 infographic.

Based upon 2018 publication statistics compiled by the Cooperative Children's Book Center at the University of Wisconsin-Madison, this infographic reveals the racial inequities of today's children's publishing industry. Notably, young BIPOC readers have access to significantly fewer representational "mirrors." American Indians/First Nations, Latinx, Asian Pacific Islander/Asian Pacific American, and African/African American students together constitute only 23 percent of today's primary characters in young people's literature, while White and Animals/Other protagonists constitute 77 percent. A snapshot of 2018, this infographic reflects a publication history that directly impacts the available representations teachers must choose from when selecting YA literature, whether print or digital.

Paradoxically, even in this dismal landscape, the amount of digital YAL circulating through digital media (e.g., blogs, podcasts, and social media) has exploded. So much so that locating the right intersectional representation for your classroom can feel like an overwhelming task. Furthermore, wading through digital YA culture in fan communities such as Wattpad, Tumblr, or Archive of Our Own reveals millions of self-published representations of diverse young adulthoods. Young people are creating the diverse "mirrors," "windows," and "sliding glass doors" they need (Coleman and Hall, 2019; Messina, 2019; Thomas & Stornaiuolo, 2016), and teachers are left to select the "right" text from among them. In other words, ELA educators might find themselves overwhelmed by the amount of digital YAL they find online. The abundance and rapidity with which digital YAL is generated online make it difficult to know which texts to choose and teach, and this feeling might conflict with the desire to address historical gaps that persist in today's print publishing landscape. This reality can lead educators to feel trapped between pasts of erasure, presents of abundance, and unknown futures related to diverse representation in YAL. Text selection in today's digital era poses new challenges to teachers, and the feelings that result can be, in a word, paradoxical.

Critically, this paradoxical feeling can upset even the most seasoned ELA teachers' text selection and make "know[ing] the literature" (*Preparing Teachers*, 2018)—one of this book's focal position statement recommendations—challenging. Well-intended yet overwhelmed, teachers are likely to return to the comfort of "tried and true" texts—ones they know they can teach with success—and these, more often than not, reinforce a white, Western canon that neglects the critical affordances of digital YAL and digital YA culture. What might change if teachers took the courageous step of embracing the paradoxical feeling of text selection in today's digital era? Could a focus on digital YAL and its surrounding culture help teachers create a more diverse and decolonized or un-whitewashed curriculum? (For more on un-whitewashing curriculum, see chapter four.) Some of the questions teachers who take on the challenge of navigating digital YAL today might consider in order to "know the literature" (*Preparing Teachers*, 2018) include:

- In the midst of rapid shifts in content and access to digital YAL, how do teachers know which texts to select for their classrooms?
- How do we simultaneously address both historical gaps in YA publishing and the overabundances of representation in digital YAL culture?
- How do we embrace the feeling of paradox around text selection in order to disrupt canon and pursue antiracist teaching in ELA?
- What role might digital YAL, especially texts produced by student authors rather than commercially published authors, play in teachers' text selection? How can student authors restory classroom texts?

In this chapter, we address the paradoxical feeling of text selection in our twenty-first-century digital age. Specifically, we demonstrate how restorying text selection—in essence, reimagining how we choose digital YAL in today's digital world—can guide teachers toward antiracist pedagogy that seeks to decolonize ELA. To illuminate this process, we spotlight the #DisruptTexts movement as one mechanism through which to "know the literature" (*Preparing Teachers*, 2018) and detail how to reimagine text selection using the #DisruptTexts' four core principles. Contributing author and former high school English teacher Coyote Shook (they/them) then presents a curriculum map for teaching speculative fiction, or "Spec Fic." Spec Fic refers to a genre of literature that departs from perceived reality, including fantasy novels, science fiction short stories, and more. Shook spotlights this genre to provide educators with a pathway for embracing YA's speculative features using digital tools. Together, this chapter provides ELA educators with concrete strategies for embracing the feeling of paradox when selecting digital YAL to teach. Today's digital world can feel overwhelming, and this is true whether teachers consider themselves to be adept digital mavens or online novices. This chapter provides a pathway for finding comfort in paradox and will show teachers how to restory text selection using digital YAL and digital YA culture.

Section 1: Restorying through Disrupting Text Selection: Teachers Speculating beyond Paradoxical Feelings

Addressing representational equity in today's digital era, #DisruptTexts began in May of 2018 as a social media hashtag by four women of Color. Tricia Ebarvia, Lorena Germán, Kimberly N. Parker, and Julia Torres (2020) sought to "advocate for a more inclusive and restorative curriculum and pedagogical approach in English Language Arts" (p. 100). Since 2018, #DisruptTexts has grown into a national movement with regional affiliates in areas such as Colorado, Virginia, Chicago, St. Louis, and more. Readily accessible online, these affiliations provide resources for disrupting ELA—everything from genre to canon itself—and can be found at disrupttexts.org. Furthermore, to unify the #DisruptText movement, the cofounders provided four core principles to support teachers as they integrate digital YAL into their classrooms using the hashtag (see Figure 2.2).

Taken together, these core principles guide a movement that is, as the founders describe, "a crowdsourced, grassroots effort by teachers for teachers" (Ebarvia, 2021). Propelling this effort, ELA teachers and librarians have taken up this invitation to #DisruptTexts using digital YAL and digital YA culture, and they have turned specifically to Twitter to do so.

This hashtag, started on Twitter, boasts a healthy social media stream, and the grassroots orientation of the movement in particular has integrated with digital YA culture. For instance, the @DisruptTexts feed often features teacher and librarian posts. On June 11, 2020, for example, @EdiCottonQuilts (librarian and YA expert Edi Campbell) wrote, "As corners of American [sic] begin purging their souls, are we going to talk about the role of children's books in the perpetuation of biases and racism?" (see Figure 2.3).

FIGURE 2.2. #DisruptTexts' core principles.

In other instances, YA authors Renée Watson and Matt de la Peña posted about #DisruptTexts to promote the selection of texts that center BIPOC representations. Together, librarians, teachers, and authors have created a living stream of digital YAL recommendations, each of which disrupts the traditional whiteness of the colonial canon (Toliver & Hadley, 2021). Such efforts live out the cofounders' idea that "liberatory work must be collective work" (Ebarvia, 2021), and #DisruptTexts feeds are invaluable guides for novice and veteran teachers alike to navigate the paradoxical challenge of text selection. Notably, this hashtag can help teachers in at least these two ways: (1) to navigate the abundance of representations that already exist and choose texts that challenge the larger historical gaps in YA

FIGURE 2.3. Screengrab from #DisruptTexts Twitter feed.

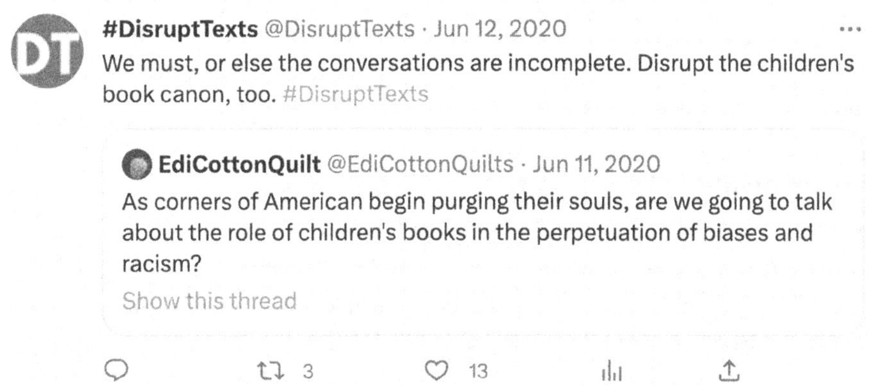

publishing and (2) to identify where gaps still exist and creatively imagine how to work with students to fill those gaps.

In the remainder of this section on disrupting text selection, we provide concrete strategies for doing so and answer the question: What might restorying text selection look like in practice? To illustrate this, we draw from Josh's restorying project with queer and trans educators to demonstrate how teachers can use the four #DisruptTexts principles to guide restoried approaches to text selection, doing so to emphasize the importance of queer and trans narratives to the #DisruptTexts project. We then explain how such restorying practices can help ELA teachers navigate those feelings of paradox created by digital YA culture today.

Speculating with Digital YAL: Queer and Trans Speculative Composing Practices

As part of a research project entitled *Restorying Painful Histories* (RPH) (Coleman, 2020), Josh invited a group of nine queer educators to "restory" past personal experiences of queerphobia (i.e., a painful history of their choosing). Over the course of a year, these educators explored this question: How might speculative storytelling or imagining how things could have been otherwise support queer educators as they address their own painful histories? Using YA literature as mentor texts, members of the group wrote narratives and then restoried identity, place, mode, perspective, metanarrative, and time in their narratives in order to reimagine how their painful history might have been different. Over the course of the year, Josh saw how restorying provided a tool for reimagining queer and trans representation. It was a narrative process that helped these participants repair the wounds of the past, and he recognized this as highly applicable to navigating the paradoxical feeling of text selection in today's digital era.

In this section, we show how findings from Josh's study can help teachers and their students answer the following question: How can teachers use restorying to #DisruptTexts and reimagine text selection using digital YAL? To facilitate this process, we explore each of the four core principles referenced above for their restorying potential and include a "Text Selection Reflection" section to guide teachers as they bring these core principles into their classroom text selection practices.

Core Principle 1: Interrogate Our Own Biases

Described as a call to action, the first #DisruptText core principle instructs teachers to "*continuously examine our own biases to understand how they inform our teaching*" (Ebarvia et al., 2020, p. 100, emphasis in original). This principle is of particular importance for text selection, as it can disrupt teachers' nostalgia for canonical literature and thus allow teachers to come to know a wider range of texts (e.g., "know your literature" [*Preparing Teachers*, 2018]). Scholars of children's and young adult literature have pointed out that nostalgia often leads teachers to teach the same texts they were taught (Nel, 2017). However, by interrogating their biases, teachers might learn to recognize those feelings that undergird their text selection, particularly those rendered invisible by subconscious nostalgia for a colonized and "All-White" literary past (Larrick, 1965).

For Josh's research participants, reimagining was central to moving beyond nostalgia and toward composing new narratives for queer and trans communities. For instance, participant Coyote (they/them)—yes, the same as this chapter's contributing author!—came to recognize they had never "considered the possibility" of writing a happy ending to any of their reimagined stories. This was a reality they shared at the conclusion of the research project (Post-Interview, 05/06/2019, Coleman, 2020). Discussing that reality, Coyote expressed,

> It just did not occur to me to make this a happy ending, and I think that is part of the thing. For all the lamenting I do that we never get happy endings as queer people, in terms of our media and our content, damn, is it hard to write happy queer endings that don't feel fake.

None of the participants in Josh's study (including Josh) had been introduced explicitly to queer and trans representation in K–12 schooling, and as expressed in *The Dark Fantastic* (Thomas, 2019), our childhood imaginations developed around such absences. These absences forged an "imagination gap" that shaped both what we imagined and, ultimately, what stories and representations we ushered into our classrooms. In other words, because the participants did not see queer stories in their own schooling, they were less inclined to usher queer stories into their own classrooms. And in Coyote's case, because they had never seen queer stories with happy endings, they were less inclined to imagine and write them into existence. As the project demonstrated, our imaginations are shaped by the representations we had access to in childhood.

Imagination gaps such as these highlight the need for teachers to question the biases we imagine into existence and bring into our classrooms as well as how nostalgia shapes our text selection. Indeed, we must come to recognize, as the first #DisruptTexts core principle explains, that "[n]o educational space is free from bias or inequity" (Ebarvia et al., 2020, p. 100). Speculation, in particular, allowed the queer educators in Josh's study to recognize the nostalgia that shaped queer and trans representations in their own childhoods. So, these participants began to restory the white supremacist, ableist, cis-heteronormative values held in their own imaginations and, critically, how these values were perpetuated through their text selection. Similarly, ELA teachers of various identities might speculate outside of their nostalgic feelings. We must question what feels comfortable as equally as what is discomforting when we select texts, and from that point, we might come to know the literature and then restory the inequitable representation we often unknowingly bring into our classroom.

Text Selection Reflection for Core Principle #1
• What texts do I remember warmly from childhood and from my own schooling? Why do I have those warm feelings about those texts? • Do I tend to teach texts that were taught to me? Which ones and why? • Who is and who is not represented in these texts, and how might this indicate an imagination gap impacting my own text selection? • How would I teach these texts differently—perhaps more critically—if I didn't feel as fondly about them? • Does digital YAL provide needed representations that can address gaps in representation caused by my own nostalgia?

Core Principle 2: Center Black, Indigenous, and Voices of Color in Literature

The second #DisruptTexts core principle calls for the centering of BIPOC authors and stories in literature, and to that we might also add queer and trans BIPOC narratives. Specifically, this principle is anchored in the call for counter-narratives or stories written to challenge dominant social narratives, and as Ebarvia et al. (2020) explain, counter-narratives allow teachers "to address harmful and problematic narratives and stereotypes that exist in society and offer students the knowledge and information to dismantle those ideas" (p. 101). We believe reading and writing counter-narratives is just as important for teachers as they illuminate imagination gaps that shape how and what YAL we teach (Thomas, 2019, p. 6). Moreover, creating counter-narratives that center BIPOC authors and stories corresponds with restorying perspective, one of the six forms of restorying (for more on these six forms, see chapter one). For Josh's participants, writing counter-narratives allowed queer educators, both of color and white, to restory painful experiences of queerphobia that shaped their willingness to be out and to even teach queer texts in the classroom. In line with #DisruptTexts' call to center BIPOC voices, Carlos (he/him) restoried an experience of queer hate speech that took place while he was visiting family in Mexico. Restorying the first-person perspective of his painful history, Carlos reimagined this story from the perspective of his great aunt and uncle's house—the location where the hate speech was uttered. Reimagining the scene from that perspective, Carlos crafted a counter-narrative that challenged the classism and homophobia contained within that space.

In line with Ebarvia et al. (2020), Carlos's restory provided a narrative through which Josh's inquiry community could address "the stereotypes that support oppression" (p. 101). For teachers, reading counter-narratives that center BIPOC experience, particularly queer of color narratives, and inviting students to write such counter-narratives to the stories they read can "change our thought patterns so that we can see each other in healthy and unbiased ways" (ibid). While non-BIPOC individuals should be leery of writing harmful representations and likely should shy away from composing BIPOC representation altogether, reading and discussing counter-narratives can help teachers to recognize and confront "our racialized imaginations by dismantling racist patterns of thought" (p. 101). After reading digital YAL, individuals in Josh's study read, discussed, and composed counter-narratives that addressed the intersection of racism and homophobia (Johnson, 2017; Muñoz, 2009; Wargo, 2018), and through restorying together, we were able to locate and challenge imagination gaps related to various intersections of queer BIPOC representation.

Moreover, restorying provides a springboard for developing text sets that intentionally challenge white supremacy, queerphobia, cisnormativity, and ableism. As teachers, you might take up this challenge of finding books with perspectives other than yours and your students', and be sure to create text sets that center BIPOC representation. Such work provides a focus for ELA educators when navigating the paradoxical feeling of text selection. Specifically, you can search for #Counternarratives and #Counterstories that highlight intersectionally diverse BIPOC, queer, and queer of color perspectives. Usefully, digital YAL located in digital YA culture is replete with divergent representations that can, indeed, disrupt the whiteness of the traditional teaching canon. Using hashtags—such as #BIPOCYA, #NativeYA, #QueerYA, #TransYA, #BlackYA, #AsianYA, #OwnVoices, and #DiverseYA to name but a few—can help teachers navigate digital YA culture in search of the digital YAL needed in their classrooms. Moreover, in the simultaneous absence and overabundance of diverse representation in digital YAL, it provides a focal point through which to "know the literature" (*Preparing Teachers*, 2018) and mitigate the perhaps anxiety-provoking, paradoxical feeling of text selection today.

Lastly, despite publishing increases in diverse representation, teachers are unlikely to find every intersectional "mirror" to your students' identities. Quite simply, the world is still diversifying, and some representations have yet to be written. So, when you can't find a needed representation, create space for your students to imagine and write their own "mirrors" into existence (Bishop, 1990). They can create the BIPOC queer, trans, disabled, transnational representations we English teachers need to address the imagination gaps that continue to influence text selection.

Text Selection Reflection for Core Principle #2
• Are BIPOC voices central, not merely an add-on, to my ELA curriculum? • Do I have multiple stories for the BIPOC communities represented in my curriculum? Have I avoided "single stories" of any BIPOC community (Adichie, 2009)? • Have I intentionally selected counter-narratives to the DWGs ("Dead White Guys") who have traditionally constituted the English literary canon? • How have I used digital YAL by (not merely about) BIPOC creators as counter-narratives in my ELA curriculum? • Have I invited my students to write counter-narratives that challenge the limitations of my curriculum and text selection?

Core Principle 3: Apply a Critical Literacy Lens to Our Teaching Practices

The third core principle drives home the reality that power is never absent from teaching YA literature, whether digital or print. Stories matter; representation matters; and the histories that surround them matter. The social contexts we teach in precede us as teachers, and for English teachers, those contexts have been steeped in racism (Baker-Bell et al., 2017) and colonization (de los Ríos et al., 2019). Per the #DisruptText founders, "[d]eveloping a critical lens means not only identifying new knowledge but also being conscious of the social, cultural, and political contexts in which that knowledge exists" (Ebarvia et al., 2020, p. 101). This reality emphasizes that teaching a text about a person of color, a queer person, or a queer and trans, disabled immigrant of color is never enough. We must critically examine *how* we teach any text. The contexts we imagine and respond to through our selection of both primary and supplementary texts impact the valences of power we reveal. In other words, while a text's content might lend itself to equity-oriented understandings of race, gender, and sexuality, both teachers and students might fail to read that text in ways that illuminate the injustice represented in the text and, then, connect those texts to their lives. Instead, coupling text selection with critical lens can invite readings that reveal the histories of racial, gender, and sexuality-based oppressions that #DisruptTexts challenges.

As we select texts, align them with critical lenses, and embed them in our ELA curricula, we must also be aware of the stories we do not tell and especially those we actively unimagine. In the third session of Josh's project, Ari (they/them), a white nonbinary individual, coined the term *de-storying* to illuminate a collective fear that we were unimagining Indigenous perspectives from our discussion of a queer YA short story, "Roja" (McLemore, 2018). Distinctive from an unintentional omission, de-storying refers to the habitual, often subconscious removal from the imagination of communities, their stories, and their histories. Written by queer and trans author Anne-Marie McLemore (they/them), "Roja" restories the "Little Red Riding Hood" fairy tale by centering queer Indigenous and trans characters. As participants shared their responses to the text, a conversation unfolded concerning whether or not the text was actually a reimagined fairy tale. Some participants worried that interpreting the text as "Little Red Riding Hood" would mean applying a Eurocentric framework to a text that centered representations of queer indigeneity and white transness. Ari, bringing the discussion to a head, said,

> When we were talking about these issues of how to read and am I reading this text correctly when I read . . . "Little Red Riding Hood" into the text? . . . I think that de-storying is a good term to identify that fear that you all were talking about because you were saying how, "Oh I don't want to read it wrong." (Ari, Session 2A, 12/02/2018, Coleman, 2020)

Specifically, Ari is referring to a fear discussed by multiple participants that they were enacting a colonizing reading of the text by imposing the "Little Red Riding Hood" framework onto it. Shaping the remainder of the discussion, de-storying called attention to the role histories of Westernized and racialized reader responses (Borsheim-Black & Sarigianides, 2019; Coleman, 2021) played in our reading and, by extension, teaching; it has become a normal reading practice to erase BIPOC, queer, trans, and disabled narratives from our interpretations of texts. This reality emphasizes the importance of critical lenses for providing interpretive frameworks related to race, queerness, gender, ability, and their intersections that combat de-storying.

We teachers must be careful of the de-storying practices we enact, and applying a critical lens can reveal the stories we are actively unimagining from consciousness through the texts we select and teach. As Appleman (2015) advocates, applying a critical lens to textual analysis is never singular. Instead, we must apply multiple lenses or interpretative prisms to our analysis of any text. No lens, no matter how powerful, can illuminate the workings of power in its entirety; instead, we must oscillate between interpretations in order to address our students' needs (Schey, 2017). For example, to combat the de-storying of queer folks of color, we might apply tenets of Critical Race Theory and queer theory (e.g., queer of color critique) to reimagine where queer of color community narratives might exist in the literature we teach. To support this reimagining, teachers might turn to digital YA culture and engage in digital dialogue on Twitter and blog forums to grow awareness of de-storied communities. Educators might then invite their students to apply these lenses to their readings of text. Next, students can write stories, counter-stories, and restories that center unimagined queers and people of color.

Caution: Careful attention must be paid to those students who might seek to write stories outside of their own experiences. Unless careful research has been conducted, students should write from their own experience in order to avoid harmful misrepresentations.

Text Selection Reflection for Core Principle #3
• Have I been trained to read in ways that would unimagine certain communities, even if I don't mean to? • Does the way I invite students to read a text perhaps unimagine some potential narratives within that story? • What are the critical lenses I use to illuminate BIPOC, queer, trans, and disabled narratives? • How do I invite students to take up multiple critical lenses when reading any text? • How do my writing assignments create space for students to imagine and write unimagined stories?

Core Principle 4: Work in Community with Other Antiracist Educators

In their final core principle, Ebarvia et al. (2020) assert that "the work of disruption cannot be done alone" (p. 101). Together, teachers must work in community with other antiracist educators, especially Black, Indigenous, and other individuals of color. As teachers, we can only know from our own positionality, and despite a vast amount of listening and learning, one can never know the experiences of another in their totality. Embracing community is one way to teach beyond our own partial knowledges. A white person will never experience and know the effects of racism in ways that BIPOC individuals live out on a daily basis. However, entering into communion with other antiracist educators can mitigate the potentials for harm in teaching digital YAL while also educating toward healing.

For instance, in Josh's study participants found that in restorying together, they were able to learn about queer intragroup differences, specifically by discussing digital YAL. Carlos, for instance, recounted his growing awareness of the differences between queer male experience and the experiences of queer folks of other genders (Post-Interview, 4/30/2019, Coleman, 2020). Interestingly, this awareness was verbalized when discussing digital YAL composed by youth on the online fan community Wattpad. Likewise, ELA teachers might create inquiry communities that bring together diverse educators committed to antiracist pedagogy and, together in discussing digital YAL, might imagine toward the realization of antiracist pedagogy in their varied contexts. Specifically, they might imagine the role digital YAL and digital YA culture can play in realizing antiracist teaching collectively.

For example, in searching Twitter and We Need Diverse Books for resources about *The Hate U Give* by Angie Thomas, teachers could find book recommendations, relevant interviews, teachers guides, and more that can support the uncovering of biases; provide excellent YAL recommendations by and about BIPOC communities; and offer resources (e.g., articles, podcasts, etc.) for developing critical lenses related to Critical Race Theory, whiteness studies, and more. Reimagining text selection with other teachers highlights powerful tools for realizing antiracism in schools. Beyond imagining tools, texts, and strategies for restorying all-white, all-straight, all-cisgender, all-able-bodied, all-American, all-middle-class narratives, teachers must also engage with other antiracist educators to realize what they have reimagined in their pedagogy.

Text Selection Reflection for Core Principle #4
• Do I think of antiracist pedagogy as primarily individual work? • Whom do I turn to when I need support orienting my teaching, classroom, and text selection toward antiracist pedagogy? • When was the last time I explored digital YAL and digital YA culture with fellow antiracist educators? • When I'm not sure how to be antiracist, whom do I turn to for honest feedback, support, and discussion in my teaching career?

Looking across the #DisruptText core principles, educators can see the role reimagining can play in realizing antiracist, queer- and trans-affirming, disability-conscious instruction in ELA classrooms. Central to each of these principles is digital YAL and digital YA culture. As mentioned above, text selection in today's digital era is challenging. It can summon a feeling of paradox because of the simultaneous gaps and abundances in representational diversity, and this paradox might stop teachers from making bold choices for their students. To overcome that paradoxical feeling, reimagining of the sort described here can transform into a restorying approach to text selection that provides ways of navigating alternative feelings, pedagogies, and texts related to digital YAL. Whether alone or in a community, ELA educators have a tool for addressing both gaps in diverse representation and the overwhelming abundance of resources circulating in digital YAL culture by reimagining text selection with #DisruptTexts.

Furthering our discussion of restoried text selection in today's digital era, contributing author Coyote Shook (they/them) draws upon their experiences as a former high school English educator to demonstrate how teachers might integrate digital YAL into their own ELA curriculum. Specifically, they provide units, texts, approaches, and assessments that center speculative fiction (i.e., fantasy, science fiction, horror, and more), and they demonstrate how it might be used to integrate

LGBTQIA+ content into even the most resistant of classrooms through digital YAL and culture.

Section 2: Weird Science: Speculative Fiction and Radical Possibilities of Teaching Queer Literature

Coyote Shook (they/them), PhD candidate, University of Texas, Austin

This section sutures together a unit on speculative literature as a method of teaching LGBTQIA+ literature to high school students. For our purposes in this book, speculative fiction is defined as books/films/media that take place in universes not defined by realism (such as science fiction, fantasy, surrealism, and magical realism). Why a focus on speculative fiction as we consider issues of text selection? From an aerial view, this task seems daunting. Corporate curriculum writing and educational bureaucracy certainly reinforce hierarchies of "good" literature that overly saturate curriculum maps with nonfiction and historical fiction. Speculative fiction authors who sometimes manage to be included in city and state curricula (such as Gabriel García Márquez, Karen Russell, and Margaret Atwood) typically have some sort of "validation" of the literary merit of their work (such as prestigious awards and commercial recognition). However, for teachers, fantasy, sci-fi, magical realism, and speculative fiction not only challenge the hierarchies of the "canon," but they also offer students accessible entry points to take up rigorous questions of race, gender, sexuality, ability, and justice through the plasticity of the authors' speculative universes.

Centering the malleability of gender and sexuality in queer science fiction, magical realism, and fantasy texts, this approach to teaching queer literature steps away from heteronormative tropes (such as farm boys going on quests, narratives that uphold individualism and the divine right of kings, "chosen one" archetypes, and heterosexual love plots) and challenges liberal queer texts that uphold the nuclear family and bourgeois acceptance in their narratives. This unit examines Mary Shelley's *Frankenstein,* Don Hertzfeldt's short film *World of Tomorrow,* Malinda Lo's *Ash,* Octavia Butler's *Fledgling,* and the anthology *Love after the End* as texts that introduce more sophisticated and challenging understandings of gender and sexuality in crafted universes that do not adhere to the limits of traditional narratives. This approach is, of course, only one of many effective and innovative methods of using literature and digital humanities to center questions of intersection liberation in the ELA classroom. By asking students to compare and contrast sexuality and gender in speculative universes in multimodal texts (including traditional books, films, comics, and digital media), students can think of queer people and their stories as complex, rich, and distinct from the reactionary and reductive politics of "love is love" (a trope that sidesteps queer experiences and reduces LGBTQIA+ narratives to only being worthy of celebration if they're romantic in nature) and, more significantly, imagine possibilities of intersectional, queer justice through literature.

Overview

"Oh, you'd LOVE *Game of Thrones*," a well-meaning heterosexual, cisgender friend tells me for the ten-thousandth time. "You have to watch it. It's queer."

I (Coyote) react the same way I might when people tell me I simply MUST watch *The Lord of the Rings* movies, *The Mandalorian*, or *The Avengers*, as though the richness of my daily life will suffer if I do not. I politely nod, dishonestly insist I will someday do that, and calibrate the mental gymnastics of how I can better communicate in the future that absolutely nothing interests me about the plasticity of white, cis-and-heteronormative speculative universes. I do not say that to position myself as a cynical former high school teacher with obvious solutions to complex problems, nor is this a manifesto about the radical potential of using *Game of Thrones* in the classroom (any publication of which appearing under my name should almost certainly be interpreted as a signal to the universe that I'm being held against my will). However, my frustrations as a nonbinary educator with mainstream LGBTQIA+ young adult literature walk a near-identical path with my fundamental suspicions with the world of white, cis-het fantasy and the role it plays in discourses of "queerness." While outdated depictions of sissies, stone-cold murderers, and subversive villains indifferent to human casualties in their quest for power are certainly no solution to the gaps in LGBTQIA+ representation in classrooms, the co-option of "queerness" into a charity model of teaching in which queer characters exist simply as a tool for heterosexual characters and/or readers to practice empathy and learn to "be themselves" also has serious limits to their radical potential. Furthermore, reducing queer narratives to pithy "love is love" slogans in which the pinnacle of conflict revolves around a character overcoming shame or "coming out" offers little for students when it comes to imagining futures for queer characters beyond acceptance from the very society that mistreats them. In this section, I take up the unique challenges and opportunities of centering speculative universes and speculative-based pedagogy in a high school English classroom. Centering works by Mary Shelley, Malinda Lo, Don Hertzfeldt, Octavia Butler, and the anthology *Love after the End*, this section aspires to imagine a working (and imperfect) framework of "radical teaching" when it comes to centering LGBTQIA+ literature in a high school classroom.

I must foreground this analysis by attempting a working definition of "radical pedagogy" when it comes to teaching queer content in high school English. For the purposes of this section, I frame "radical pedagogy" as one that invites critique, abolition, and replacement of oppressive systems of being (Love, 2019). Like all definitions, this, too, is thorny and riddled with caveats. The first is that I write this from a place of extreme privilege as a white teacher who worked exclusively in urban public schools with strong unions and supportive principals when it came to LGBTQIA+-inclusive curricula and classrooms. It is considerably easier to do the work of experimental education methods and incorporating texts with diverse characters in spaces where doing so will not cost you your job. Secondly, we are teaching and living in a deeply imperfect system. Borrowing from Alexis Shotwell's framework in *Against Purity,* I'm not attempting to craft a "how-to" guide, nor shame or guilt teachers who recognize the limitations of an imperfect system. For many students, books about gay penguins will provide some of the only LGBTQIA+ representation they will encounter in schools, and the teachers who bring queer texts into the classroom do so at professional and often personal risk. Instead, this is best understood as an invitation to conversation, a call to discourse about what kinds of texts we can use to teach queer content and what methods we can utilize to produce a sort of "wonderful thinking" when it comes to innovative pedagogy. By extending the definition of *literature* to include digital media, film, and webcomics and by allowing students to use digital media as a form of assessment (such as using iMovie, GarageBand, YouTube, etc.), teachers restructure the definition of a narrative and expand the understanding of queer storytelling beyond traditional texts.

The problem with liberal discourse in queerness and speculative fiction is apparent. The rise of neoliberal worldviews (which emphasize individualism, personal decision making, and the implicit good of a small government) impacted queer people in a range of ways. As Melinda Cooper (2017) notes in *Family Values,* neoliberalism rapidly changed public perception of queer people (and especially white, cisgender queer people) from impoverished, sickly, and signs of urban decay from the peak of the HIV/AIDS crisis to wine-sipping, cardigan-wearing, monogamous couples who gleefully gentrify neighborhoods and have no problem getting loans from banks. Achievements like same-sex marriage and other tokens of queer "citizenship" in a post-Reagan America rhetorically serve to emphasize an imaginary tolerance of a perpetually "self-improving" capitalism and a belief that nebulous concepts like "empathy" and "inclusivity" are inherently better for queer people than abolishing the very forces of patriarchal capitalism that oppressed us in the first place. Picture books for young children illustrate these challenges. Texts like *King & King, And Tango Makes Three,* and *Worm Loves Worm* craft fantasy universes in which social constructs like marriage, the nuclear family, and even the concept of an antidemocratic monarchy are not challenged. For queer characters, the happy ending is integration into neoliberal citizenship in which some antagonist (portrayed as an easily won-over traditionalist) comes around in the end.

For young adult queer literature, the universes of traditional texts are likewise unimaginative. Queer characters are almost invariably trapped in "progressive" narratives that center monogamous relationships and acceptance from a previously hostile entity. To some degree, digital texts (such as fan-fic, digital comics, web video parodies, and TikTok videos) on their own do not necessarily act radically in their politics. Fan-fic and "restorying" might pair Harry Potter and Draco Malfoy in a romantic relationship without Draco's racism or Harry's unbearable personality undergoing changes. Webcartoonists might make transgender girls win beauty pageants. Amazon Prime might release a film about lesbians fighting for the right to go to prom together. A white boy in an exclusive prep school with no personality beyond gayness and wealth finds love and eventually becomes United States Secretary of Transportation. The extreme limitations to these literary universes become quickly apparent. If the goal of those stories is ingratiating protagonists into white dominant, cis-heterosexual acceptance, it is fundamentally antiradical to the liberative justice a speculative universe might offer. Why, teachers might ask, do we center beauty and "passing" as the only happy ending for transgender girls? Why might going to the prom uphold not only materialistic values but also center monogamous relationships as an acceptable gateway to cis-heterosexual acceptance? Speculative universes that de-center white-dominant, cis-hetero acceptance likewise de-center the damaging values of that framework.

Approach to Texts

I (Coyote) frame this section with a sample curriculum map. This outline of a year-long course on speculative fiction and LGBTQIA+ storytelling is merely meant to be a framing device that can and should be adapted to individual schools, departments, and classrooms. The texts were selected based on previous use with students in my own teaching and were selected to include various intersections of race, sexuality, gender, and ability in terms of authors and content creators." It is certainly not exhaustive, and teachers should feel comfortable adding or removing texts that would speak to their own classroom demographics and expertise. While it does assume students in the class would have access to computers and Apple apps, it should be viewed more as an invitation to dialogue and collaboration than as a firm guide. For teachers in classrooms without access to such technology, inviting students to be collaborative partners in talking about the kinds of technology they use outside of school could be a useful gateway for students. Assigning them to imagine or create fictional "digital spaces" that might be useful for sharing information might also be a useful practice. Teachers might simply use the *Frankenstein* section of this map for a single unit, for example. Or they could condense units one and two into a single unit and examine speculative fiction as a genre using *Frankenstein* as the core text. It is an extremely malleable proposed text map in that regard, and units within it have the freedom to stand alone if the teacher is unable to dedicate an entire year to speculative literature or experimental texts due to district-wide regulations or departmental restrictions.

TABLE 2.1: Curriculum map.

Unit One "What Is Speculative Fiction?"	**Unit Two** Weird Science: *Frankenstein* and the Queer Birth of Speculative Fiction	**Unit Three** Fairyland: Restorying and Magic	**Unit Four** Toward Intersectionality
Core Text *World of Tomorrow* Don Hertzfeldt **Supplemental Texts** Advertisement for *Orlando* by Virginia Woolf (digitized artifact) "Love in a Very Cold Climate" (webcomic) Isabel Greenberg "The Debutante" Leonora Carrington "Two Houses" Kelly Link "St. Lucy's Home for Girls Raised by Wolves" Karen Russell "The Eye of the Beholder" (*Twilight Zone* episode)	**Core Text** *Frankenstein* Mary Shelley **Supplemental Texts** "A Vindication of the Rights of Women" by Mary Wollstonecraft *Frankenstein* (1931) *The Bride of Frankenstein* (1935) *The Spirit of the Beehive* (1973)	**Core Text** *Ash* Malinda Lo **Supplemental Texts** "The Bloody Chamber" Angela Carter Excerpts from *Superman: Red Son* (a restorying of Superman in which he lands as a baby in the Soviet Union instead of the USA)	**Core Text** *Fledgling* Octavia Butler **Supplemental Texts** *Love after the End* edited by Joshua Whitehead *The Urgency of Intersectionality* Kimberlé Crenshaw (TED Talk)
Summative Assessment Students will analyze a work of speculative children's literature (picture book, film, or an excerpt from a longer novel) and analyze it through a queer lens. Does the text challenge gender and sexuality in a meaningful way? Why or why not?	**Summative Assessment** Students will write a synthesis paper comparing the themes of gender, sexuality, and science in Mary Shelley's book *Frankenstein* and Victor Erice's 1973 film, *The Spirit of the Beehive.*	**Summative Assessment** Students will work in teams to create a queer "restorying" of a fairy tale/myth/folktale and produce a movie trailer for it using iMovie, YouTube, or some other digital storytelling medium. In this restorying, students must explain how sexuality and gender change from the traditional story and their "restory" and why they structured their restory the way they did.	**Summative Assessment** Students will complete a digital concept map that traces intersecting themes of gender, race, and sexuality in Octavia Butler's *Fledgling.* Students will then construct a paper analyzing the theme of intersectionality in Butler's speculative universe.

Essential Questions	**Essential Questions**	**Essential Questions**	**Essential Questions**
What is speculative fiction? What does the word *queer* mean? Is this distinct from "gay and lesbian" literature? Why might speculative fiction have historically appealed to queer authors?	How does Shelley challenge and/or adhere to traditional understandings of sexuality? What role does science play in defining our understanding of sexuality and gender? Are there limits to that framework? What does science fiction offer queer writers when it comes to challenging traditional views of gender and sexuality?	Why might authors restory rather than construct a new story from scratch? What are the benefits of restorying versus creating new universes? How do the authors' restorying of fairy tales challenge gender and sexuality? What themes from the original stories do the authors seem to be challenging? What role does magic play when it comes to understandings of gender and sexuality? How is it different from how Shelley and other speculative authors might use science?	Why might intersectionality be an important lens for queer people of color, queer disabled people, and other multiply marginalized people? What does Butler's universe offer in terms of queer representation that others do not? How might Butler have written this text in 2021? How might she write it in 2050? Would the categories of identity she constructs be different? Similar?

With those caveats noted, my focus begins with Don Hertzfeldt's short cartoon film *World of Tomorrow* and the impending apocalypse in a clone-populated universe in which love can exist between aliens, humans, robots, and even inanimate objects. This digital text introduces students to key questions about the possibilities of a speculative narrative that does not necessarily restrict itself to the limits of scientific knowledge and physics. A mere fifteen minutes long, the comical, poignant cartoon traces three-year-old Emily visiting with a clone of hers from 200 years into the future. Coming from a techno-dystopian future in which memories and personalities are electronically transferred from clone to clone from an original source, the future Emily tells her original source (or Emily Prime) about the world of tomorrow. Love and affection are not defined by heterosexual confines. The future Emily falls in love with rocks, robots, aliens, and, eventually, an ill-fated clone named David. Though short, the dense film serves as the bedrock upon which students can examine how speculative futures can imagine sexuality and gender. Teachers might ask how characters do or do not "act" like their assigned gender, how Emily's romantic relationships are portrayed, and how the world of cloning complicates ideas of romantic love. Essential questions for this unit ask student to specifically take up the question of speculation, science fiction, and magic when it comes to examining sex and gender as fluid and shifting.

In addition to Hertzfeldt's film, students also read speculative fiction short stories from several genres (including magical realism, science fiction, and surrealism). Throughout the unit, it is prudent and necessary for teachers to have conversations with students about what feminist and queer literary analysis means. As many students in the class might not be queer or might not be women, it is vital to walk students through the process of what thoughtful and sensitive approaches to queer and feminist scholarship might look like while centering that queer people and non-male people are not theoretical but are humans who stand to be harmed if the analysis is done improperly. Modeling this task can be useful for students. For example, a teacher might use the children's book *The Paper Bag Princess* by Robert Munsch to show students what a feminist reading of the text might include while also explaining to students the arguments queer readers have made that the text is homophobic. Furthermore, it is useful to talk to students about their own assumptions regarding queer and feminist storytelling. What sorts of "happy endings" do students imagine for queer characters? What about non-male characters? What values are embedded in those assumptions of a "happy ending"? As a summative assessment, students self-select some form of children's media (such as a picture book, cartoon, digital story, webseries, etc.) that takes place in a speculative universe and conduct a "queer reading" of it, assessing how the text depicts gender and sexuality through a speculative lens. What constructions of gender and sexuality does the text disregard or challenge? What are the implications of those challenges and changes? How does the removal of gender and sexuality norms impact other literary devices like plot, theme, and character development? Possible texts include *Steven Universe, Adventure Time,* and Anderson's "The Little Mermaid."

In the next unit, students then examine early speculative fiction in Mary Shelley's *Frankenstein,* in which asexual reproduction is possible through the power of science. Her own sexuality the frequent source of speculation, Shelley and her iconic *Frankenstein* offer multiple lines of inquiry into queer literature and the radical possibilities of speculative universes, including the queer 1931 film *Frankenstein* and its sequel *(The Bride of Frankenstein)* directed by the openly gay James Whale and the 1973 Spanish film *The Spirit of the Beehive.* This unit offers particularly useful possibilities for teachers constrained by more rigid curriculum demands, as *Frankenstein* has largely achieved canonical status in English literature and is likely to appear on Common Core and Advanced Placement recommended text lists. However, despite the trappings of canonical status, the text is particularly useful when it comes to tracing the history of speculative literature and how Shelley's work transgressed both gender and sexuality norms in 1817 England. This unit, focusing primarily on close readings of the text, requires formative assessments of a close reading analysis paper of a chapter of *Frankenstein* and a scene analysis of the 1973 film *The Spirit of the Beehive.* Using YouTube, students practice a "scene analysis" by using cinematic technique terminology (such as use of sound, shot, and cinematography) to make an argument about how the director is approaching themes of sexuality, gender, etc. Finally, students write a synthesis paper and compare the themes of gender, sexuality, and science in a scene from *The Spirit of the Beehive* to a close reading of a passage from its source material in Shelley's *Frankenstein*.

In unit three, a case study of the author or of her work *Ash* offers possibilities of "restorying" or taking a familiar text and rewriting it to change the outcome. Lo's queer retelling of "Cinderella" reimagines the romance as being between a lesbian teenager named Ash and a huntress named Kaisa, keeping the basic structure of the text but presenting alternative understandings of romantic and physical attraction in a more complex fantasy universe. Students are introduced to the concept of "restorying" through a reading of "The Bloody Chamber" by Angela Carter, itself a feminist "restorying" of the Bluebeard fairy tale. Students discuss why restorying might be a useful tool for LGBTQIA+ storytellers. Framed as an un-essay, the assessment for this unit involves students working in groups to present a queer restorying of a fairy tale, myth, or folktale, including character analyses, a description of how gender and sexuality function in the original story as well as the "restory," and how the "restory" offers a different ending for queer characters. As part of their final assessment, students turn their story into a movie trailer using iMovie, YouTube, or some other digital storytelling device. As students are completing this task, they consider how their retelling follows the framework of #DisruptTexts. How is retelling a story a form of disruption? How do the changes students made to the source material disrupt meaning? What does disruption offer readers in terms of imagining a more just and liberated world?

In unit four, students examine queer speculative fiction through an intersectional lens. Centering the work of Octavia Butler, this unit requires students to apply Crenshaw's principles of intersectionality to Butler's speculative universe. Students ask themselves how categories of gender, race, ability, and sexuality function in the world she constructs in *Fledgling* and how she writes against white-dominant narratives in science fiction. Students read critiques of white-dominant narratives in speculative fiction from authors such as N. K. Jemisin and Sami Schalk that challenge narrative structures that center ruralism, the divine right of kings, and an erasure of race, queerness, and sexuality through white cultural colonization in those speculative universes. As with unit one, it is useful and helpful in the framing of this unit to discuss BIPOC literary analysis and framing a strong lens for students to think about how authors describe and use race in their texts. As before, it is essential for teachers to discuss that the implications of racism are not abstract and cause real harm to BIPOC people. Students, in turn, analyze queer-of-color speculative universes through a similar lens. Students examine short stories from *Love after the End: An Anthology of Two-Spirit and Indigiqueer Speculative Fiction* using Crenshaw's intersectionality framework. As a summative assessment, students complete a digital concept map using Lucidchart, Whiteboard, or another digital medium that traces the intersecting themes of gender, sexuality, and race in Butler's queer vampire novel *Fledgling*.

As previously stated, this curriculum map is designed to be an invitation to collaboration. Sidestepping the political aims of many queer texts that center mere recognition or tolerance from cisgender and heterosexual readers, queer speculative fiction does the work of asking readers to imagine the prospect of queer liberation and justice. Rather than position queer characters as objects of sympathy for cis-het readers, these texts likewise invite readers to speculate. In constructed universes that need not adhere to liberal humanist values, political constructs, or even scientific principles, what kinds of lives and stories can we imagine for queer characters, particularly queer characters of color? Rooted in multimodal texts that often uncomfortably fit (or even fail to fit) within traditional literary forms, the texts themselves disorient forms and standard conceptions of genre. Furthermore, requiring students to engage in the process of restorying, speculative analysis, and deconstructing literary themes in complex texts demands rigorous analytical skills and the ability to read texts through different lenses but also invites students to approach literature from a political lens that empowers students to think critically about a liberated, justice-centered world.

Conclusion

In this chapter, we, alongside our contributing author Coyote Shook, have addressed the paradoxical feeling of text selection relative to digital YAL and digital YA culture. In today's digital era, there are simultaneously historical gaps in representation and an overabundance of representations online that make it difficult to "know the literature" (*Preparing Teachers*, 2018). To navigate this felt sense of paradox, we aligned restorying with the four #DisruptTexts core principles: (1) interrogating our own biases, (2) centering BIPOC stories, (3) applying critical lenses, and (4) working in community and, based on Josh's research project, highlighting restorying as a means to reimagine text selection and navigate the felt sense of paradox elicited by text selection today. As the focal NCTE position statement of this book asserts, "Preservice teachers should cultivate book knowledge . . . [and] build knowledge of resources—including review journals, websites and blogs, [and] social media discussion" (*Preparing Teachers*, 2018). Digital YAL and digital YA culture contribute to this project by providing pre- and inservice educators with tools for "knowing the literature" (*Preparing Teachers*, 2018). Through digital resources, teachers can restory their text selection and navigate the paradox of today's digital era.

Also in this chapter, Coyote shared a malleable ELA unit about speculative literature and demonstrated the importance of teachers embracing the speculative—of imaginatively exploring what could be—for questions of social justice. Specifically, they explore how queer, trans, and BIPOC representations that are unrestricted by realism allow readers and writers to imagine and feel worlds free of homophobia, transphobia, racism, settler colonialism, ableism, and more. Tied to digital YAL, such speculation gestures toward restoried worlds that provide emotional sustenance for navigating the realities of today, and these worlds can be located by navigating digital YA culture through hashtags and disrupting texts.

In summary, text selection in a digital era functions differently, and by reimagining text selection, we can embrace the overabundance of digital YAL to address histories of misrepresentations and come to "know the literature" of today's digital era (*Preparing Teachers*, 2018). Harnessing the present, we can, indeed, heal the past while also restorying teachers' paradoxical feelings toward text selection. However, this responsibility is not one ELA educators could or should bear alone. Instead, educators might turn to other members of their school, neighborhood, and national communities to navigate the paradoxes of teaching in today's digital era. In chapter three, "Restorying Digital Access," we demonstrate this truth by spotlighting librarians as vital access builders to digital YAL and digital YA culture for both students and teachers.

Chapter Three

Restorying Digital Access: Youth Librarians as Access Builders in a Digital Era

> *The first step in understanding the [digital] paradigm shift in school and public library services for and with teens is to look at who teens are today. We begin by putting their lives within the context . . . that is causing perhaps the most disruption for all libraries, for education, and for society overall—technology . . . it is probably the most pervasive element causing a need for a shift in library services for and with this age group.*
>
> (Braun et al., 2014)

Digital technology has changed what it means for students to study YAL in the twenty-first century, and as discussed in chapters one and two, even what counts as YAL is changing. Ever in reach, cell phones provide many students with instant access to streams of literary content, including life narratives, speculative fiction, and more. Thus, in today's digital era, the role of teaching and learning is changing, and teachers' charge to "be readers" who lead "literate lives" (*Preparing Teachers*, 2018) has grown increasingly complex. ELA teachers now confront unprecedented quantities of youth literature that is easily held in the palm of one's hand, and this shift in both amount and access to YA literary content demands a pedagogical skill set that can adapt (Perillo, 2017). The COVID-19 pandemic reinforced this reality by highlighting the challenges and the potential of digital YAL—

for instance, the tenuous divide between in-person and remote learning. In short, digital technology is redefining what counts as YAL, how teachers teach with YAL, and even where learning with YAL takes place.

To meet the demands of our digital era, teachers of all levels must recognize the limits of our pedagogical training to animate learning around YAL in today's digital age. Frankly, most teacher training has focused on in-person learning and less on digital technology's role in driving ELA instruction. Addressing this reality, in this chapter, we demonstrate how ELA teachers are not alone in the fight to teach digital YAL. Fortunately, educators have experts to turn to, individuals who are specifically trained to navigate digital technology, information or literary content overload, and the integration of digital YAL and digital YA culture in K–12 classrooms. Teachers today are so fortunate to have youth librarians, and as this book's NCTE position statement advises, ELA educators must "invest in relationships with librarians" (*Preparing Teachers*, 2018).

Whether located in schools, communities, or online themselves, librarians and specifically youth librarians bring their knowledge and training to the table yet are seldom integrated in ELA classrooms to their fullest potential. We authors believe that youth librarians are key not only to teaching with digital YAL but to achieving equity in today's schools. Youth librarians support ELA teachers to navigate today's information-rich, online learning environments and to provide pedagogical tools for integrating digital YAL and digital YA culture into our classrooms. Together, librarians and classroom teachers can "affirm diversity and exercise critical literacy" (*Preparing Teachers*, 2018) by confronting one of the greatest inequities for teaching and learning in the digital era—access.

The connections between today's digital landscape and issues of equity are, of course, complex. Since the late 1990s, questions of access have been central to teaching and learning with digital technologies, and most often, these concerns have surfaced in discussion of a so-called "digital divide" (Rowsell et al., 2017). Positioning learners as the haves or have-nots, early discussions of the digital divide brought much needed attention to assumptions regarding who did and did not have physical access to the internet and technology. In its limited focus, however, this scholarship perpetuated false narratives about certain communities of learners. As Tisha Lewis Ellison and Marva Solomon (2019) point out, African American students have been falsely depicted—through both Google Image search algorithms and media narratives—as wholly without physical and skill-based access to technology. Troubling this narrative, Ellison and Solomon demonstrate the sophisticated ways in which African American families harness technology to read and write themselves into existence. For example, they trace how parents and students use digital technology (e.g., cell phones, iPads, and video games) to craft counter-narratives in their *Dig-A-Fam: Families' Digital Storytelling Project* and, in so doing, demonstrate the potential of embracing digital

YAL to augment ELA learning in classrooms. Moreover, the digital divide has been tied to socioeconomic status, rurality, and able-bodiedness in ways that, without careful consideration, can perpetuate that early binary of the haves and have-nots. Learning in today's information-rich environment is not a light switch, and students do not simply have or not have access to the internet and technology. Youth librarians are central actors in troubling false narratives related to the digital divide and, by extension, digital YAL and digital YA culture.

Troubling these narratives does not imply, however, there are no challenges in today's schools. Challenges deeply rooted in histories of equity and access shape how and which students come to be supported—or not—through digital learning. As the "From Good Intentions to Real Outcomes" (Reich & Ito, 2017) report details, access to digital materials and learning, including YAL, circulates around three primary challenges in today's schools:

1. ***Same Technology, Unequal Schools:*** *Schools serving privileged students tend to use the same technologies in more progressive ways than schools serving less privileged students.*
2. ***Open ≠ Equitable:*** *Free online learning materials disproportionately benefit the affluent and highly educated.*
3. ***Social and Cultural Forces Derail Good Intentions:*** New technologies are taken up in varied and unexpected ways by diverse learners and in diverse settings. *Once technological and economic barriers are removed, broader social and cultural forces determine outcomes.* Efforts to democratize education through technology have often faltered because technologists failed to anticipate broader social and cultural forces. Unintended outcomes commonly grow out of two underlying social and cultural forces: *institutionalized and unconscious bias and social distance between developers and those they seek to serve.* (p. 3, emphasis in original)

Youth librarians are central to combatting each of these challenges in schools. In their role as information experts, youth librarians create networked access between teachers, students, and communities in order to navigate the "divides" that surround digital YAL. This chapter focuses primarily on librarians' potential to address the report's third point—*Social and Cultural Forces Derail Good Intentions.* We see this as the most pivotal in challenging the deleterious narratives and inequitable access surrounding digital YAL and digital YA culture.

We believe youth librarians are "access builders" between students, teachers, and communities. They are experts who can teach ELA teachers pedagogical tips, tricks, and tools to navigate today's information-rich environment using digital technology. In this chapter, we demonstrate how librarians provide access to digital YAL and digital YA culture through (1) community building in and beyond schools, (2) skill building for students and teachers, and (3) motivation building. Written in two sections, this chapter's first section, written by contributing author Latrice Ferguson (she/her), offers an overview of current practices in schools and public libraries and includes firsthand accounts of youth programs both in and out of school spaces. She also provides anecdotes from school and community librarians of how they have used digital YAL with students as well as suggestions for how teachers might engage their librarians to challenge issues of equity and access in today's digital era. Section 2, written by the primary authors Josh, Autumn, and Ebony, provides insight into a number of initiatives by youth librarians that center diverse, digital YAL and its surrounding digital YA culture. Primarily, we focus on the #ReadWoke initiative by award-winning youth librarian Cecily Strong and the Blogging for Access initiative as mechanisms for teachers to "be readers" (*Preparing Teachers*, 2018). Furthermore, for each initiative, we provide classroom connections that detail pedagogical strategies and activities that integrate digital YAL into ELA classrooms.

Taken together, the sections in this chapter provide teachers with the conceptual and pedagogical tools to become access builders themselves as they "affirm diversity and exercise critical literacy" (*Preparing Teachers*, 2018). By building access to digital YAL, educators can honor students' sociocultural legacies and current realities by working in tandem with youth librarians, locally and across the United States. Expanding limited conceptions of the "digital divide," this chapter foregrounds youth librarians as access builders who restory those deficit narratives surrounding the haves and have-nots along lines of race, class, gender, and more. In our estimation, youth librarians are key to realizing justice in the face of a "digital divide" preserved by inequitable social and cultural forces, and these forces are deeply embedded in the history of a racist, classist, and ableist nation. It's time to restory the digital divide by increasing access to digital YAL and digital YA culture with the aid of youth librarians.

Section 1: Facilitating Digital Futures in the Classroom and Beyond: Youth Librarians and the Multiple Roles They Play in Schools and Communities

Latrice Ferguson, PhD candidate, University of Pennsylvania

It's been over a decade since the American Association of School Librarians (AASL) released *Standards for the 21st Century Learner in Action*. As schools across the country began to adopt the national Common Core State Standards, AASL similarly sought to implement national standards for school library instruction, and the association developed standards intended to encourage learners by developing their multiple literacy skills and teaching them to navigate the growing information landscape. At that time, school librarians and school library programs' growing mission looked toward that new landscape and associated digital technologies and wanted to develop "critical thinkers, enthusiastic readers, skillful researchers, and ethical users of information" (AASL, 2009). While the mission and purpose for school libraries has not changed, the standards and tools have significantly developed over the course of the last decade due largely to digital technologies and greater access to information. The new AASL standards are attuned to the fact that literacy learning connected to digital YAL happens both within and beyond the doors of the classroom and that school libraries can be dynamic, collaborative spaces for both students and teachers; libraries fuse text and technology, and patrons utilize their own ways of reading and writing in their interactions with them (Kapitzke, 2001). Beyond that, school libraries can be inclusive places that offer students opportunities for independent inquiry and reading. School librarians, throughout library school, learn that collaboration and partnerships with teachers and administrators grow library programs and thus are primed to support student learning through building access.

Unfortunately, school library programs across the country are among the first to be cut when budgets get tight. As mentioned above, equal access to technology is sometimes without programs that encourage exploration and develop tech knowledge. The loss of school library programs in rural and urban school districts can be a major contributor to that inequity and to ongoing narratives of the digital divide. As suggested in the "From Good Intentions to Real Outcomes" report (Reich & Ito, 2017), among the greatest barriers to integrating the digital in schools are the inequitable distribution of materials and unequal access for students most in need. School districts across the US have seen significant cuts to library programs and certified school librarians. In California, the librarian to student ratio is 1:7,034 (Ahlfeld, 2019). Chicago has seen their school libraries shuttered and librarians cut from 454 in 2013 to just 108 full-time librarians in 2019 serving a school district of 514 schools (Carlton, 2016; Inklebarger, 2019). Studies, including thirty-four statewide studies, have shown that student reading and literacy test scores are better in schools with high-quality library programs and skilled librarians (Gretes, 2013; Lance & Kachel, 2018). Despite the growing data, cash-strapped urban and rural school districts that serve poor and racially diverse student populations continue to see decreases in school library programs (Bamberger et al., 2020; Graham, 2020). Often with ever decreasing budgets, school librarians work alone in school buildings.

Being alone in their building can make advocating for themselves and their work as access builders an uphill battle. It can be especially difficult for school librarians, who often juggle multiple roles and responsibilities including collection development and maintenance, library tech upkeep, teaching responsibilities, and taking care of the physical library space while also finding time to sit in on department meetings to collaborate with teachers. While many teachers may value their school librarians, there are still some who do not trust the expertise of their librarians, many of whom were once classroom teachers. There are likely ELA teachers interested in collaboration but who are not sure how to begin and sustain collaborations with librarians. Digital YAL and digital YA culture provide great avenues for exploration, and youth librarians, as evidenced by the new AASL standards, are trained and attuned to the growing tech landscape.

A great way to open the doors of communication between teachers and librarians is to consider the multiple hats your school librarian must wear. In what follows, I provide vignettes and firsthand knowledge from current school librarians that demonstrate the potential of collaborations around digital YAL and digital YA culture to build readers and affirm diversity (Buehler et al., 2018). These vignettes and anecdotes are organized by the multiple hats school librarians wear: *Teacher-Librarian*, *Media Specialist*, *Reader Advisor*, and *Information Literacy Advocate*.

School Librarians as Teacher-Librarians

Beyond their ability to function in the library, many librarians are highly qualified to do work within the classroom. Teacher-librarian "denotes a professional with dual teaching and library qualifications and, where applicable, includes school librarian, school media specialist, etc.; teacher-librarian is hyphenated to indicate the interconnected elements of the dual role" (Hughes, 2014, p. 30). Their dual role as teacher-librarians means they not only know how to utilize new technologies but have the skills to communicate and share that information with students. Additionally, many librarians have classroom experience prior to beginning their journey into the library role. Their classroom experiences often inform their library practices in ways that could make collaboration in the school library easier. Collaboration with school librarians around digital YAL can look a variety of ways, from teaching a unit on searching for materials and citing sources to faculty professional development featuring new technology, materials, and resources provided by the library (Gardner, 2020). The skills students learn make them more effective learners and are useful throughout their lives (Hughes, 2014). Those skills include the navigating of "fake news" and misleading information sources but also helping students become more efficient researchers and source explorers, more responsible users of technology, and more thoughtful global citizens, who harness digital YAL and culture for social justice.

Words from a Teacher-Librarian

Gretchen Zaitzeff
School Librarian, New York

As collaborative partners with classroom educators, school librarians can lift a lesson or unit to a whole new level, engaging students in their learning and relieving teachers of the entirety of the instructional development. It is not unusual for a teacher to reach out to a school librarian to help them find resources, but as a school librarian, I can do so much more to assist teachers and their students. When approached by a world literature teacher about finding resources for a lit circle unit, I offered my expertise as a co-teacher in developing a unit that highlighted graphic novels written by authors representing six of the seven continents. At the appropriate points in the unit's timeline, I taught students about the history of comics and how to read them, including format-specific vocabulary. Then I introduced students to the LibGuide I created for the unit, book-talked some of the titles available to them, and helped them obtain their reading choices. The classroom teacher led the lit circles and whole-class discussions based on our instructional objectives. Toward the end of the unit, I taught the students how to use an online tool to create their own comics, telling the stories of their cultural heritage. Together, the classroom teacher and I provided students with a unique learning experience that culminated in new ways to communicate and connect with the global community, their family histories, and their own stories.

Five Ways to Use Your Teacher-Librarian

1. Often a teacher might ask a teacher-librarian for a booklist in support of a unit. Consider asking a teacher-librarian to do an engaging book talk about the collected items or a digital YAL text.
2. Consider collaborating on a lesson using digital storytelling and epistolary novels. Ask a teacher-librarian to introduce digital editing tools and digital storytelling techniques that parallel the ways epistolary novels develop narratives. Titles to consider: *Gabi, a Girl in Pieces* by Isabel Quintero, *The Color Purple* by Alice Walker, *The Perks of Being a Wallflower* by Stephen Chbosky, *Dear Justyce* or *Dear Martin* by Nic Stone.
3. Geo-mapping converts data into visual maps. Classroom teachers and teacher-librarians can develop a lesson to help students visualize data from digital YA novels read in the classroom and their relationships to the local, national, and international. For example, you might use *Dear Haiti, Love Alaine* by Maika and Maritza Moulite to map both the current and historical references in Haiti and add additional context.
4. Similar to geo-mapping, create digital timelines to help students visualize the relationship between novels and their relationship to real life events. Consider *The Hate U Give* by Angie Thomas and mapping a timeline of the novel and its parallels to recent protests movements in the aftermath of George Floyd's

death. Also consider timelines that compare historical fiction with records of historical events. Teacher-librarians can help students sort through primary resources and news databases.

5. Lastly, consider just sharing lessons you're thinking of revitalizing or new lessons with your teacher-librarian that center digital YAL and culture. They might have skills and insights to help you get the ball rolling.

School Librarians as Media Specialists

School libraries have typically functioned as both a library and the school's technology outpost. As technology was integrated into school curricula and devices like laptops and iPads were introduced to students, libraries housed those materials and learned how to use them. Funding through the Elementary and Secondary Education Act (ESEA) and Knapp School Library Project supported updating libraries and adding technology to support students across the country (Wine, 2016). A survey of school library use during the COVID-19 pandemic highlighted all the ways school librarians have played vital roles in online teaching and student support. In their effort to increase equity and access to digital technology, many schools have charged librarians with developing media resources and support for students. Librarians have recorded read-alouds of digital YAL for teachers struggling with Zoom lesson planning. One teacher, Liz Goldfarb at Booker T. Washington Junior High School in New York City, asked her students for help managing the new digital tech and teaching their peers how to use it (Witteveen, 2020). The pandemic shocked the world; everyone had to adjust to the new safety guidelines, and school librarians, just as much as their teacher and administrator peers, rose to the challenge.

Words from a Media Specialist

Mary Thomas

District of Columbia International School

During the online and hybrid learning portions of the pandemic, I worked really closely with our director of technology and media. I think one of the most important things we did to support teachers and students was to provide digital organization strategies and training. One thing we focused on with teachers was the layout and organization of their Google classrooms. The use of topics, common naming conventions for assignments, and a weekly syllabus with an overview of the work that would be covered with time estimates for independent work helped students find their classwork and understand what was expected of them each week. Another support for teachers was encouraging them to use sites like bit.ly and tinyurl.com to make important links (like their Zoom rooms) easy to memorize/access. For both teachers and students, we encouraged the use of bookmark folders on Chrome, as well as OneTab to help organize collections of tabs/links specific to certain classes or sections. In addition to the tools themselves, we offered individualized support to teachers. Both the director of tech and I were available for Zoom meetings/virtual office hours, offered filmed screencasts, and provided asynchronous training and slide decks for teachers to access on their time.

Five Ways to Use Your Library Media Specialist

1. Find out if your librarian offers tech tours for teachers and students.
2. Ask your librarian for a demo of technology offered in the library that addresses digital YAL.
3. Investigate with your librarian the online resources, tools, hardware, and software you might use in your classroom to support teaching digital YAL and digital YA culture.
4. Set up a time with your librarian to give you and your students a tour of the school library's digital space and any relevant online catalogs.
5. Ask your library to share any resources about digital YAL and digital YA culture that seem underused.

School Librarians as Reader Advisors

Libraries offer so much more than books as media, and reading materials are broadly central to a library's collection. Across Twitter and Instagram, librarians vocally #ReadWoke, #DisruptTexts, and promote #OwnVoices that center digital YAL and its culture in order to support students and teachers to "be readers" (*Preparing Teachers*, 2018). They build library collections that both support the curriculum and delight readers. However, navigating the library for even the most avid reader takes time and knowledge. In *The Reading Teacher,* Paige Green (2018), a teacher-librarian in Illinois, frequently writes that "students often do not have strategies to help them find books on their own. I see them frantically checking out the first book they find, or they wander the fiction section, overwhelmed because they do not know where to start" (p. 404). Librarians can teach students the skills necessary to navigate libraries and are likely prepared to talk about the newest materials they have read or purchased for their collections. Digital YAL projects that librarians have used to support student readers include creating zines, book trailers, and book reviews for social media platforms.

Words from a Reader Advisor

Julia Torres

Denver Public Schools

Whenever students work up the courage to request help finding a book, I know that is an invitation. It is an invitation to peek into the windows of their lives and identities. It is an invitation to help take part in shaping what their reading lives will look like now—and perhaps forever. When we are invited to play a part in anyone's story, it is imperative we remember how difficult it can be to practice vulnerability, especially when it comes to owning reading proficiency. In our library, we are fortunate to have access to a robust physical library collection in addition to our extensive online library. During the global pandemic when all learning happened at a distance, we leaned heavily on the online library and virtual book clubs to continue to engage readers. However, it was extremely difficult to be distanced from my physical library, as so much of my teacher identity has been tied to being in that specific place.

Now that we have returned, it is quite exciting to see that, though students are glad to be reunited with physical books, they are equally comfortable using the online library. Students are also able to build and maintain community by participating in a virtual book club, because we have eight different bell schedules for the five schools on campus, and it isn't feasible to get everyone together in one place at one time to hold discussions unless we think differently about our time and how to use it. So many different online platforms for accessing literature have evolved out of the past decade, and I am grateful to be a librarian in an age when readers can use digital platforms to increase font size, annotate texts, access read-alongs, listen to audio books, and watch videos on YouTube of their favorite authors reading aloud. All of these modalities have made connecting readers with great books so much easier, even those who have fallen off or otherwise exited the reading train, which is common in the secondary levels of education. I like telling them, "You can get back on at any time. The station isn't going anywhere" almost as much as I like seeing the looks on their faces when they accept the invitation and step onboard.

Words from a Reader Advisor

Erika Schmidt

Chicago Public Library

I had two patrons who used our library space to start their own business. Twin brothers first learned how to use the vinyl cutter we had in the space; once they found out we had heat transfer vinyl and a heat press to put it on t-shirts, they got super-excited. They would come in almost every day to use the vinyl cutter and heat press in order to make shirts for themselves and friends. Then, they started selling them! While they became better and better at using the equipment, I started to recommend YA books about entrepreneurship and managing a business. They began to bring their own materials and utilize the equipment more and more! It was exciting (but we did need to remind the teens to share the space and the equipment with others)!

Five Ways to Use a Reader Advisory Specialist

1. Ask a school librarian to do book talks for classrooms to promote new library books and materials around digital YAL when those materials arrive or early in the school year.
2. Collaborate to create book trailers or online book reviews for digital YAL titles read in class or read independently by students to post and share online.
3. Many cities and states have book awards that local students can help select. Ask a librarian how students can begin participating in that process.
4. Consider taking a tour of the library early in the school year to learn how to navigate the collection and its organization. Ask about passive ways librarians offer readers advice around digital YAL like genre stickers, displays of similar novels or series, nonfiction/fiction pairings, and organizing the collection by genre.
5. Create a book club (if your school does not have one) to encourage students to utilize the library and its materials that focus on digital YAL and digital YA culture.

School Librarians as Information Literacy Advocates

Neil Gaiman infamously asserted that "Google will bring you back, you know, a hundred thousand answers. A librarian will bring you back the right one" (Potter, 2016, Threats Section). While that sentiment helps illustrate the value of librarians, however, it is far more accurate to say librarians want to teach you to find the most useful source as efficiently as possible. Teaching students (and patrons, for public librarians) how to navigate, evaluate, and ethically utilize materials about digital YAL is a key aspect of librarianship. A study by the Stanford History Education Group in 2020 found that two-thirds of the students they surveyed from a large East Coast state university could not decipher an article's trustworthiness (Valenza, 2020; Wineberg et al., 2020). Unfortunately, as the study indicates, students still struggle to navigate online resources. The recent US Capitol insurrection illustrates how easily people can be swayed by misinformation. School librarians have long worked in collaboration with teachers on inquiry-based learning projects. As technology has expanded, research papers have become one option among many for students to illustrate and share their work. Digital YAL projects like YouTube videos, interactive timelines, social media hashtag campaigns, and online mapping offer students a variety of ways to share information.

Words from an Information Literacy Advocate

Latrice Ferguson

One of the best experiences I had as a librarian was setting up a QR code scavenger hunt during the Freshmen Program's orientation week. It was a fun and engaging way for students to learn the library's online and offline spaces. Through this activity, the ninth graders learned to search the library's online catalog to find both fiction and nonfiction titles. To find the books on shelf, they got to explore the organizational system the library used to make finding books easier. Additionally, the scavenger hunt led to other online databases they would eventually use to search for articles for their research papers. Lastly, ninth graders met the library staff and learned how we could be a research resource for them or a great book recommender. As the year went on, I worked closely with the teachers in the program to provide more in-depth lessons on how to search online databases and websites, tools for citing sources, and navigating the local school, public, and university libraries.

Five Ways to Use Your Information Literacy Advocate

1. Invite your librarian to demonstrate how students can identify fake or misleading news sources about digital YAL.
2. Ask your librarian to share tips and tricks to help your students navigate online resources using Google, Google Scholar, and a library's online catalog, especially when beginning their projects.
3. Have your librarian facilitate learning about why citing sources is important and also how to cite sources from digital YA culture findings.
4. Set up a time for your librarian to lead tutorials about finding primary sources and navigating the elements of a digital YAL book (table of contents, index, etc.).
5. Find out from your librarian about LibGuides or other resource lists that students can easily access to dive more deeply into digital YAL research.

Beyond and with the School Library

If you do not have a school library or librarian, there are still library resources and skilled professionals available to you in the form of local public librarians serving youth. Unfortunately, as mentioned, well-equipped school libraries are frequently absent in schools that serve the most vulnerable populations; however, public libraries also promote access and support with digital YAL for teachers and youth. Across the country, programs like the YOUmedia Learning Labs (youmedia.org) and youth library programs offer opportunities to create, explore, and engineer. YOUmedia promotes

HOMAGO (hanging out, messing around, and geeking out). Youth can access the materials in the space and just explore. There are music studios, film equipment, sewing machines, and 3D printers in various YOUmedia and other library makerspaces across the United States. The action happening in makerspaces can include creating a podcast, making a movie, recording a song, and much more (Good, 2013; Moorefield-Lang, 2015; Slatter & Howard, 2013). Libraries are offering up spaces and teaching youth how to make their voices heard as they and their teachers read, write, and navigate digital YAL and digital YA culture.

As budgets decline in schools and cities, librarians find themselves constantly urging stakeholders to recognize the value librarians bring to schools and communities. Beyond that, youth librarians advocate for and elevate the voices of children and teens by inviting teachers to read books both by and about them. Unequal access, misinformation, and sociocultural barriers make it more difficult for librarians to meet the needs of students. Despite those barriers, however, youth librarians have remained committed to the ideals of building access to digital YAL as promoted in the AASL Standards for School Librarians. Beyond the classroom, public youth librarians continue to create inclusive and welcoming spaces for independent learning. Because of this, public library spaces are becoming increasingly useful resources for ELA teachers. As in-school libraries continue to close across the US, youth library spaces have been filled with technology to support integrating digital YAL and its attendant digital YA culture into learning both in and beyond the classroom. Together, librarians and ELA teachers might guide their young patrons toward autonomous learning as they read, write, and access digital YAL.

Words from a Public Librarian

Rashael Apuya
Public Librarian, Manhattan, KS

In partnership with programming and outreach librarians, the teen services librarian at the Manhattan Public Library currently provides virtual programs for tweens and teens. The library offers its Summer Reading Program, which encourages teens to read up to ten hours throughout June and July and to claim incentives; over 400 teens currently participate in the 2021 Summer Reading Program. I, with input from teens, create book displays to promote new and noteworthy titles in the young adult collection. I also offer readers' advisory in-house as well as online through our Personalized Reading List service that allows patrons to request a reading list be curated for them by a librarian based on their interests and reading history. We have been hosting an Among Us virtual program that allows tweens and teens to play with other local teens in a safe online space. And in March and April, we will be adding *Dungeons & Dragons* virtual sessions for older teens. Teens are also encouraged to attend our combined adult and teen programs that include fun crafts and topical book discussions. We also have a virtual teen advisory board to determine what the teens want to participate in and how we can facilitate that online.

Section 2: Woke Youth Librarians: Creating Access to Diversity through Digital YAL Initiatives

Run by youth librarian K. T. Horning, the Cooperative Children's Book Center (CCBC) out of the University of Wisconsin-Madison publishes annual statistics about shifting representational trends in children's and YA print literature (CCBC, 2020). Notably, these statistics reveal a bleak though changing landscape of diverse representation. David Huyck and Sarah Park Dahlen's infographic discussed in chapter two reveals gross inequities between representations of BIPOC characters and white/animal/other characters. Likewise, Reflection Press's Maya Gonzalez and Matthew SG (2022) have drawn upon these same statistics to spotlight inequitable publication access for diverse authors (see Figure 3.1). Their infographic accounts for "books missing by POC/Indigenous authors" for the 2015–2017 time frame, and it illuminates an alarming trend in which books "about" BIPOC individuals have increased while books "by" BIPOC authors have not. In gross, authors are increasingly writing racially diverse characters whose lived experiences differ from their own.

FIGURE 3.1. Radical Act US publisher infographic.

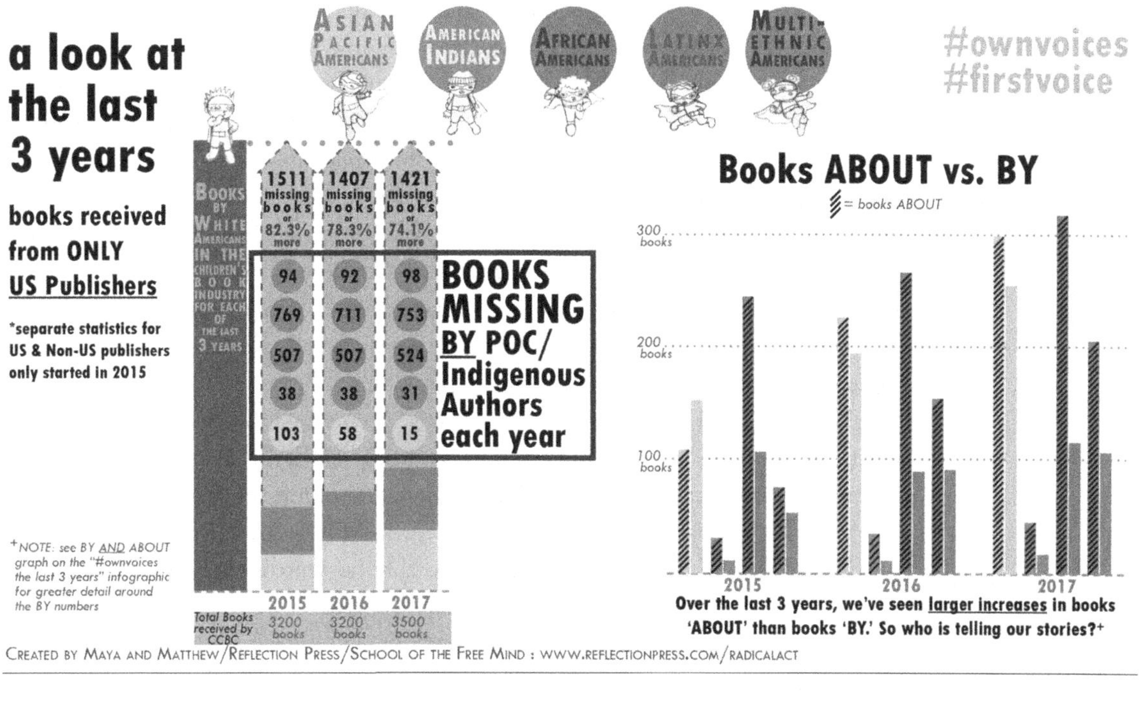

Such publication disparities have been challenged by the #OwnVoices movement. Begun by Corrine Duyvis (2021), #OwnVoices was created "to recommend kid lit about diverse characters written by authors from that same diverse group," and it has pressured the publication industry to adopt equity approaches to publishing historically marginalized authors. As important, #OwnVoices has significant limitations that foreground the challenges of identity politics (e.g., is a Mexican American author writing a Guatemalan narrative #OwnVoices if both author and character identify as Latinx?). Regardless, #OwnVoices continues to function as a useful litmus test through which to advocate obtaining access for authors often barred from the publication industry. Noting again this alarming representational landscape, youth librarians are leading the charge online to change such statistics. In this section, we primary authors spotlight some of the exceptional initiatives by youth librarians who are using digital YAL to reshape the representational statistics above. We then provide "classroom connections" ELA teachers might use to "affirm diversity and exercise critical literacy" (*Preparing Teachers*, 2018) while also increasing access to digital YAL and digital YA culture in their classrooms.

Initiative 1: #ReadWoke

Created and led by award-winning youth librarian Cicely Lewis, #ReadWoke began in November of 2017 in response to a world in crisis (Lewis, 2017). Addressing current events head-on—from pervasive policy brutality to the challenging of transgender rights to the repeal of DACA and the so-called "Muslim ban"—Lewis crafted a media initiative that centered digital YAL. Remixing the StayWoke edition of *Essence* magazine, she created a movement in which young people would #ReadWoke YA books and then complete a reading challenge (See Figure 3.2.). After reading a YA book of their choosing, students then described and recommended it online as a woke text. As Lewis (2017) describes, "Read Woke is a movement. It is a feeling. It is a style. It is a form of education. It is a call to action. . . . It means learning about others so that you can treat people with the respect and dignity that they deserve no matter their religion, race, creed, or color." Centering historically marginalized communities, the #ReadWoke movement has since exploded across digital platforms from Instagram to Twitter to YouTube and has been taken up by libraries across the country.

Notably, "Read Woke Across America" has become a nationwide movement. Dovetailing with the National Education Association's (NEA) Read Across America program, Lewis introduced #ReadWoke to address recent revelations about Dr. Seuss's (Theodor Geisel's) racist depictions of Black, African American, Asian, Asian American, Arab, and Muslim communities. Notably, he wrote these both before and during his career as a children's literature author (Ishizuka & Stephens, 2019). While the original Read Across America program had often built itself around Dr. Seuss's

FIGURE 3.2. #ReadWoke challenge.

work, Read Woke Across America recommends diverse picture books to support ELA teachers in "be[ing] readers" (*Preparing Teachers*, 2018) and to teach English language learners, students with disabilities, queer and trans students, and more, and as Lewis (2019) rightly points out, "picture books can be used with high school students too." #ReadWoke has expanded what counts as digital YAL and has provided access to diverse print and digital texts—from picture books to YA novels—and all are useful for teaching about digital YAL and digital YA culture in secondary contexts.

Furthermore, Twitter is abuzz with #ReadWoke. Even a quick search on Twitter demonstrates the impact of the movement. You can scroll for hours and see the incredible work youth librarians are doing across the country. They are providing access to digital YAL for young people, adults, teachers, and communities, while also inviting teachers to take up the "transformative activist stance" needed to "exercise critical literacy" (*Preparing Teachers*, 2018). Namely, librarians from across the country are sharing woke texts in pursuit of "arming [students and teachers] with the knowledge to protect your rights" (Lewis, 2017) while also centering "respect and dignity" for all. For her efforts, Cecily Lewis was awarded the 2019 National Teacher Award for Lifelong Readers from the National Council of Teachers of English (NCTE) and Penguin Random House (PRH) as well as the 2020 School Librarian of the Year award presented by the *School Library Journal (SLJ)* and sponsored by Scholastic.

Classroom Connection 1: #ReadWoke Text Selection

Young adult literature is a genre constantly in flux. It responds to the needs of young people and our contemporary world by providing new representations that often circulate through digital YA culture. The responsiveness of the genre also resists forming a canon and thus complicates teachers' ability to select the "right" text for our students.

#ReadWoke provides a way for students to sift through the expansive possibilities of text selection and become readers (for more on this, see chapter two). One way it does this is through a list of "Criteria for Reading" woke texts (Lewis, 2017). As Lewis explains, woke texts must:

- Challenge a social norm
- Give voice to the voiceless
- Provide information about a group that has been disenfranchised
- Seek to challenge the status quo
- Have a protagonist from an underrepresented or oppressed group

Moreover, #ReadWoke, because it is an online movement, provides digital YAL recommendations live, and these address the shifting political climates surrounding young people's lives.

YA literature should be chosen based on the needs of the students you are teaching, and it should respond to students' worlds—to the sociocultural and historical realities in which they live, this being true for local and global contexts both past and present. For teachers, #ReadWoke provides a livestream across platforms, from Twitter to Facebook to Instagram, and youth librarians across the country are recommending digital YAL in real time. Teachers can review these recommendations and determine a text's relevance to their own teaching context in ways that support taking up a transformative activist stance. Namely, #ReadWoke supports ELA educators to "recognize that they are always learning" and to "open to guiding difficult discussions about inequity with students" (*Preparing Teachers*, 2018, Recommendations Section). Moreover, #ReadWoke texts are often cross hashtagged with other selection criteria such as #WeNeedDiverseBooks, #Disability, #NativeAmericanHeritageMonth, and more. Following these hashtags through digital YA culture might also provide useful texts for students as they affirm diversity and engage critical literacy.

Classroom Connection 2: #ReadWoke Lesson Plans and Learning Activities

While woke YA texts can be used for Silent Sustained Reading (SSR) or integrated into a classroom library, students also need intentionally crafted lesson plans and learning activities to illuminate the impact of these texts upon their lives. Cecily Lewis provides a Google Drive with instructional supports for teachers; these are intended to increase students' knowledges of their rights while centering respect and dignity for all people. The link to Lewis's Google Drive is https://tinyurl.com/ReadWokeGoogleDrive and includes the following:

- Commercial for #ReadWoke
- Before and After reading graphic organizer
- Nonfiction graphic organizer
- Create your own READ WOKE protest sign activity
- Read Woke Bingo
- Read Woke Activities and Lessons
- Read Woke Book Tasting
- Read Woke Certificate
- Read Woke Bookmarks

While great places to start reading woke, these resources should be tailored to students' sociocultural and academic needs, to the context of teaching and learning, and to the representation or themes afforded by a woke text. Additionally, Pinterest has provided a crowdsourced, teacher- and youth librarian-led collection of teaching strategies teachers might use to #ReadWoke in their own classrooms. One Pinterest URL of note is www.pinterest.com/dlflee/read-woke/, which has been curated by user Dawn Foster.

Initiative 2: Using Digital YA Culture to Blog for Access

Youth librarians are also using digital YA culture to increase access for YA aficionados. They are doing this through a number of blogs that provide booklists and teaching resources relevant to any classroom. Debbie Reese, a tribally enrolled member of the Nambé Pueblo nation, helps run the *American Indians in Children's Literature* blog. Focused on representations of Native people, the website provides information including annual "Best Books" from Native authors, general resources for learning and teaching about Native life, and even a list of "Problematic Phrases" to structure discussion around YA texts (Reese & Mendoza, 2022). Likewise, Edi Campbell of the *Crazyquiltedi* blog provides resources for bringing BIPOC/NA (Black, Indigenous, people of color, and Native American) authors to the fore in pedagogy about digital YAL. As she explains, her blog is meant "to make IPOC authors and their works more accessible, to make all the pieces fit together [like a quilt]" (Campbell, 2010). Campbell's blog provides an annual booklist by IPOC authors, suggestions for "Coming of Age Movies," diversity resources, and links to POC/NA young adult authors. These are only two of the incredible blogs youth librarians are using to promote access to diverse representations in digital YA—their work is intended for ELA teachers and aligns with the four recommendations of this book's NCTE focal position statement (for more, see chapter one).

Again, the digital era is defined by a proliferation of information and the subsequent "digital divide" of access. While that access does refer to physical access to the internet and technology, it also refers to critical teacher skills and pedagogical knowledge to navigate data-rich digital platforms, archives, and databases about digital YAL. The internet can be an overwhelming place. However, youth librarians are blogging access pathways into existence, and these provide a treasure trove of vetted digital resources, activities, and other pedagogical tools to integrate diverse, digital YAL into your classrooms. Here are a few additional blogs either created by youth librarians or that use librarianship to share resources relevant to digital YAL:

We Need Diverse Books (www.diversebooks.org/)	Resource for advocacy efforts around locating and teaching diverse books.
Build Your Stack (www.ncte.org/build-your-stack/)	NCTE (National Council of Teachers of English) resource share to support teachers in expanding their knowledge of diverse books.
Booktoss (www.booktoss.org)	Blog by Dr. Laura Jiménez that encourages tossing books that are problematic.
The Conscious Kid (www.theconsciouskid.org)	Education blog focused on healthy racial identity development.
Reading While White (www.readingwhilewhite.blogspot.com)	Blog by white librarians to support white readers in embracing diverse books.
Lee and Low (www.blog.leeandlow.com)	Publisher blog that explores race and other forms of diversity in education.
Reading Spark (www.readingspark.wordpress.com)	Blog by Dr. Sarah Dahlen that focuses on Asian/Asian American representation.
Disability in Kid Lit (www.disabilityinkidlit.com)	Blog focused on disabilities representation.
YA Pride (www.yapride.com)	Blog focused on LGBTQIA+ representation in young adult literature.
Latinx in Kid Lit (www.latinosinkidlit.com)	Blog focused on Latinx representation in kid lit

Classroom Connection 3: Digital Detectives Blogging into the Future of Research

In a different NCTE position statement, *Definition of Literacy in a Digital Age*, the committee that generated the report writes that "the internet is one of the primary information sources of the modern era, making it a necessity for learners to understand how to participate and navigate the networked world" (Witte et al., 2019). In our information-rich digital age, even what counts as an academic resource is changing. Blogs helmed by youth librarians are invaluable resources for teaching, learning, and researching digital YAL. In his university YAL courses, Josh has invited students, most of whom are preservice ELA teachers, to become "digital detectives" and explore a personal, critical inquiry related to digital YAL. First, students generate a tentative, critical inquiry question and discuss their potential inquiry in a group. They then draft a formal research question such as, "How have representations of queer people of color in YA changed in the twenty-first century?"

Often students have trouble with the right "grain size" of these research questions. Thus, group feedback helps students weigh out the possibility of answering their research question prior to diving into research. These future educators then transform into "digital detectives," and Josh provides them with a list of vetted blogs (much like the list provided above) to begin their research into digital YAL via the digital YA culture surrounding it. Through their own exploration, students typically come to realize the value of blogs curated by youth librarians, professors, and other YAL experts. Ultimately, students share their findings with their groups and the class and then use that research to develop a paper or project that centers digital YAL and their own critical inquiries and literacies. To cap off the activity, Josh facilitates a discussion about the role blogs play in providing access to high-quality, vetted representations of historically marginalized communities, and he foregrounds these resources as necessities for cultivating culturally and historically responsive classrooms (Muhammad, 2020). Finally, the "digital detectives" process can be easily tailored to many learning contexts so that students might develop their research skills and even explore ethical considerations related to digital YAL. In chapter four, we detail how teachers can use "digital detectives" as a strategy to invite students into an exploration of YAL fandoms, specifically of Wattpad, and thereby increase their familiarity with navigating digital YA culture.

Conclusion

In this chapter, we have foregrounded youth librarians' pivotal role in supporting teachers to "be readers," "affirm diversity," and "exercise critical literacy" (*Preparing*

Teachers, 2018) while sharing digital YAL and digital YA culture with their students. Addressing inequities and deleterious narratives of the "digital divide," librarians are access builders who connect students, teachers, and communities with resources to navigate today's information-rich digital era. In section 1, Latrice Ferguson provided firsthand accounts from school and community librarians that detailed successful programming with and around digital YAL and digital YA culture. Furthermore, the "Five Ways to Use Your . . ." sections supplied questions and approaches ELA teachers might use to invite and sustain collaboration with youth librarians in their classrooms. In section 2, we focused on several initiatives by YAL experts and librarians. In particular, #ReadWoke illuminated the potential of digital YA culture's online networks to galvanize social change. Finally, each initiative in this section was accompanied by a classroom connection to support English teachers in bringing the library and librarianship into their classrooms.

Sadly, youth librarians and their expertise in navigating today's digital era often remain overlooked in ELA classrooms. It is high time teachers learn from and with the librarians who are sitting right next door. By doing so, teachers might more effectively harness digital YAL and culture to become access builders. Complementing the individual community members, like librarians, who support student and teacher learning, digital YAL and digital YA culture's liberatory potential is equally shaped by curricula, and historically, ELA curricula has espoused deeply held commitments to whiteness (Griffin & James, 2018). In chapter four, "Restorying YAL Curricula," we demonstrate how restorying could be used to "un-whitewash" the curricula built around digital YAL and digital YA culture.

Chapter Four

Restorying YAL Curricula: Un-Whitewashing Curricula in English Language Arts

Extending our discussion of restorying text selection and access, this chapter focuses on the ways educators can effectively restory literacy curricula for a digital age by: (1) taking up an expansive definition of text, (2) positioning students as knowledge makers, and (3) reimagining possibilities for collaborative curriculum creation with students as partners in the process. To do so, this chapter explores a process of collaborative production—curriculum creation *with* students—and the outcome of a lesson about student-guided interests. Specifically, we take up the concept of un-whitewashing digital literacy curricula in order to center and uplift students' racial identities and literacies and, furthermore, to "affirm diversity and exercise critical literacy" around digital YAL (*Preparing Teachers*, 2018). We begin with a brief theoretical overview of how literacy curricula have historically been propagated as white property and how this notion has been perpetuated in digital spaces. We then discuss the affordances of digital texts and a racialized youth lens to restory digital curricula. Then, applying this lens, Autumn details the work she did with nine Black adolescent girls at a school where each student is given a computer. We then demonstrate how teachers can integrate fandom into their classrooms in order to un-whitewash curricula, drawing upon work Josh has done in his preservice young adult literature classes. Finally, we conclude this chapter with recommendations for teachers who seek to collaborate with their students to create learning experiences that recognize, center, and uplift students' knowledge. Specifically, we detail how teachers might partner *with* students to disrupt notions of literacy curricula as white property and create learning experiences—and ultimately digital YAL—together.

Section 1: Literacy Curricula as White Property and Restorying Digital YAL

Curriculum has long been used as a means of centering and preserving the stories, lives, and achievements of middle-class, white, cisgender, straight men. The notion of whiteness as property was first penned in the writings of legal scholar and critical race theorist Cheryl Harris (1993). Her work shed light on the historical relationship between property rights and racial domination in the United States, suggesting race and property were conflated due to the nature of their relationship. Extending Harris's concept of whiteness as property, Griffin and James (2018) situated humanities curricula as white property, arguing it has been used to preserve and perpetuate white supremacist narratives and ways of knowing in both literacy and history curricula. They discussed the ways literacy curricula (1) emphasize "canonical" texts; (2) exclude the stories of people from racially marginalized populations (i.e., Black, Indigenous, Latinx, and Asian authors); and (3) misrepresent or distort the stories of racially marginalized people (see Table 4.1). Scholars have since discussed how racism is reflected and manifested through technology, including digital YAL, and how digital tools work to increase the social control of Black and Brown bodies (Price-Dennis & Sealey-Ruiz, 2021; Thomas & Stornaiuolo, 2016).

For instance, Safiya Noble (2018) takes up the term *technological redlining* to discuss the ways "digital decisions reinforce oppressive social relationships and enact new modes of racial profiling . . . by making visible the ways capital, race, and gender are factors in creating unequal conditions" (p. 1). Likewise, Haddix and Sealey-Ruiz (2012) have discussed how this redlining exists in classrooms, noting the myriad ways teachers demonize Black urban students' use of technology in classrooms. Throughout this chapter, we present models of digital literacy learning and curricula that disrupt digital literary whiteness (Borsheim-Black & Sarigianides, 2019) and technological redlining (Noble, 2018) by both taking up expansive notions of "text" (especially as it deals with the digital) and focusing on the restorying efforts of educators and young people.

Digital Texts and a Digital Racialized Youth Lens

The digital age of the twenty-first century inherently influences how young people interact with traditional texts. A 2018 Pew Research Center survey reported that 95 percent of teens have access to mobile technology and are "constantly online" (Anderson & Jiang, 2018). As youth engage online, they interact with any number of texts,

TABLE 4.1. Literacy curricula as white property.

Tenets of Humanities Curricula as White Property	Definition	Examples
Emphasizing Canonical Texts	Widely accepted "quality" texts that privilege and preserve narratives either told by middle-class, cis-het white men or denoting them as the hero or victor of the text.	• *Adventures of Huckleberry Finn* • *Catcher in the Rye* • *The Great Gatsby* • *Great Expectations*
Excluding the Stories of Historically Marginalized Populations	Erasure of a group of people from curricular texts; covertly teaches students that their history, voices, and experiences are not valued.	
Misrepresenting/ Distorting the Stories of Historically Marginalized People and/or White Saviorhood	Narratives that, when taught incorrectly, perpetuate stereotypes about a group of people; these texts are often tokenized within a curriculum.	*Black Boy*—Richard Wright *A Raisin in the Sun*—Lorraine Hansberry • When taught in isolation or without an interrogation of systemic racism, both these texts can perpetuate myths about the "Angry Black Man." *To Kill a Mockingbird*—Harper Lee • Without context, this book features Atticus Finch as a white savior.

including blogs, threads, videos, and audio presentations. Youth take up these tools for their own purposes within the context of a networked community, creating a distinct YA culture around youth and digital media (i.e., digital YA culture) that is influenced by both modality and identity (Rosenblatt, 1995). Thus, we take up a digital racialized youth lens throughout this chapter to understand how curriculum can be restoried.

Drawing on the work of Freire (1970) and other critical pedagogues, we believe texts offer students opportunities to read not only the word but also the world: *their* world. Borsheim-Black and Sarigianides (2019) take up this same notion in their ideation of a youth lens. A youth lens, they argue, "guides the study of how adolescence is depicted in literary texts. The central question of a Youth Lens is: How do texts represent adolescents/ce?" (p. 20). They further argue that adolescence is often depicted through the eyes of adults and then presented to true adolescents in classrooms. Such engagement with texts, Borsheim-Black and Sarigianides (2019) contend, denies young people dignity, authenticity, and individuality. In the same way, erasing a students' racialized identity from texts and curriculum dehumanizes them and diminishes their voices, knowledge, and brilliance (Muhammad, 2020). Just as age influences readers' interaction with and response to a text, a reader's racialized identity and the representation of it within a text informs how they understand and are able to interact with a text, especially in the digital. When we decenter whiteness within digital literacy curricula, we open up opportunities for youths' racialized reading responses and open up possibilities for disrupting technological redlining.

In the example that follows, we share work Autumn has done with a group of Black girls to use digital texts to position them as knowledge makers. Because of the digital texts we chose for the lesson, the girls with whom Autumn worked were able to draw on their racialized and gendered funds of knowledge as Black girls to create thoughtful questions that guided our literature discussion. In the next section, we offer several examples of ways teachers may be able to re-create such experiences with their students.

Discussing Colorism in the Digital with Autumn: Using Texts to Position Students as Knowledge Makers

Autumn's experience in restorying curriculum took place at a public charter middle and high school in the Mid-Atlantic region of the United States. Autumn, a Black millennial woman and former secondary teacher, served as the teacher researcher in a group of nine Black adolescent girls. The collective ranged in age from 14 to 17 and met weekly in the school library throughout the course of the semester to discuss themes related to Black girlhood, digital literacy, and self-love in a literacy collaborative. The girls were recruited for the group by their principal. Each week, Autumn and the girls would gather around a table in the library as they explored various topics related to Black girlhood through varied texts. Often, students' own out-of-school digital literacies guided our discussions, as they brought in their own digital young adult literature—the digitized texts themselves—to present to the group. Applying a racialized youth lens facilitates our understanding of how the girls' questions worked to retextualize "adult" media to focus on their own YA interests and concerns. Below, Autumn details the specific methods she used to cultivate a digital YA curriculum amongst the group.

"What is it y'all would like to discuss next week?" Autumn typed into the group chat. The group had taken to directing their own curricular choices in the collaborative learning space. As they navigated the realm of digital learning together, Autumn sought to create a learning environment that mirrored the collaborative creation process so many adolescents engage with in varied digital platforms outside the walls of the school. So far in our time together, the group had chosen to take up matters of civic literacy, healthy communication, future planning, and radical body positivity. However, a sudden change in the school's daily schedule due to testing allowed for a bonus meeting, and Autumn turned to the group to ask what it was they wanted to learn. Jazmine [pseudonyms are used for all students and schools named] quickly responded, "colorism, texturism, and navigating the world as Black women." The rest of the group quickly chimed in with variations of "yesss!" and "agreed" that let Autumn know Jazmine's suggestion would indeed be the topic for that week. Drawing on her knowledge of digital YAL, Autumn turned to media, tapping into digital YA culture and media (the participatory network of blogs, feeds, etc.) as she planned the discussion for the week.

In an effort to disrupt historically held notions of literacy curriculum as white property, Autumn drew from youth media culture and popular Black media, which served as the texts. The group began the discussion by first collectively defining both *colorism and texturism* and then watched two video clips that guided the discussion. The first, "Good and Bad Hair," a clip from Spike Lee's (1988) movie *School Daze,* features a song in which cast members deal with the politics of colorism. The second clip, "The Politics of Skin Tone" (*The Guardian,* 2019), is a video produced by *The Guardian* in which eight Black women discuss the sociopolitical effects of skin tone within Black communities. As the group watched the videos, the teens used Google Slides to jot down the questions, statements, and thoughts that would guide the discussion. Their questions included:

1. Why would Spike Lee include this song in his movie? What is the importance?
2. Do you think light-skinned people should be the ones to "open the doors" for dark-skin appreciation?
3. I wonder what light skins perceptive on colorism? [sic]
4. How can we overcome or break down the system of colorism?
5. How does colorism affect how you view yourself/your self-esteem?
6. How are black men affected by colorism, and how do they perpetuate it?
7. How does texturism exist/interact with colorism (i.e., darker-skinned women with softer hair/lighter-skinned women with kinkier hair)?
8. Did the actresses actually agree with what they were saying?
9. Did y'all notice that even the light-skin women had more ballet/polish dance move and the darker skin were more like contemporary.

After watching both videos and writing their questions, the students took a moment to read the questions they had collectively posed. Autumn then turned the discussion over to the young women, encouraging them to facilitate the discussion as they engaged the digital texts by asking and answering questions of race, gender, class, and skin tone.

Cultivating a Digital YAL Curriculum

Step 1: Determine a Topic

The first, and perhaps most involved, step to cultivating a digital YAL curriculum is to determine a topic—a matter in a text that will be taken up through discourse and/or dialogue. Engaging in digital YA culture in classrooms requires that we know and take up topics relevant to the lives of students. Selecting a topic relevant to the lives of students requires deeply knowing who they are, what issues impact their daily lives, what brings them joy, and what they care about deeply. For instance, quite often, white teachers make the well-meaning assumption that all Black students enjoy rap music and thus will create—or ask students to create—lyrics to songs to help them memorize content. While this may spark some students' interest, it is often a shallow or stereotypical understanding of Black childhoods. Determining a relevant topic that decenters literary whiteness requires an understanding of self (including one's own biases, preconceived notions, and prejudices) *and* an understanding of students; it calls for a commitment to racial literacy and decentering white curricula and ways of understanding the world.

In their recent book, *Advancing Racial Literacies in Teacher Education: Activism for Equity in Digital Spaces*, Detra Price-Dennis and Yolanda Sealey-Ruiz (2021) define racial literacy in schools as "the ability to read, discuss, and write about situations that address racial inequality and racial bias as part of the norm of schooling process" (p. 22) (see Figure 4.1). They argue that

> [i]n schools, healthy conversations on the effects of racism across class, culture, race, and other characteristics of diversity are possible. Multiple texts and modalities to engage students in these conversations are readily available through digital technologies. To develop racial literacy among students, the use of historical, fictional, poetic, and digital texts is most effective. Teachers who are able to engage their students successfully in the topic of race are most effective when they have engaged in self-exploration and honest assessment of their role in perpetuating racist ideas. Once specific behaviors are recognized, it becomes easier for the racially literate person to interrupt those behaviors in future moments and guide others to do the same. (p. 22)

As we explored in chapter two, the work of engaging in self-exploration and honest assessment of one's own role in perpetuating racist ideas begins with honest reflection about topic and text selection. The thematic units and daily lessons we plan, as well as the books and excerpts we select, say much about what we believe to be true about the world and our students.

FIGURE 4.1. Racial Literacy Development pyramid.

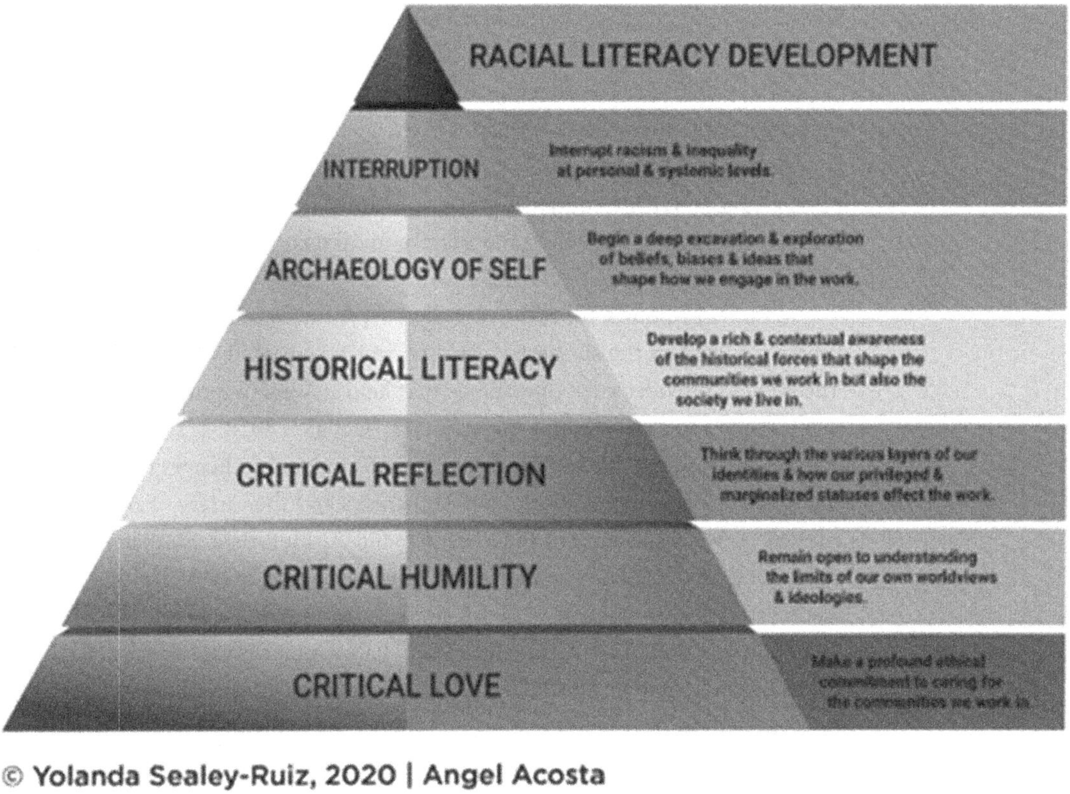

Price-Dennis and Sealey-Ruiz (2021) lay out three tenets of racial literacy development that we believe are also necessary tenets of topic selection:

- Question Assumptions: In order to develop racial literacy, teachers must (1) question their assumptions about race; (2) acknowledge their biases; and (3) assume that what they know about race is faulty and incomplete.
- Engage in Critical Conversations: Teachers must work toward and develop the confidence to discuss their concerns about teaching racially diverse content and in racially diverse settings; these conversations are an outlet for questioning un- or subconscious assumptions the individual has about race.
- Practice Reflexivity: Locating their own position influences how teachers see the world (Crenshaw, 1991). This tenet requires time to learn about the self in relation to racism and racial injustice; it is a cyclical process of (re)examination.

By developing racial literacy and engaging these three tenets, teachers are able to determine relevant topics that not only spark students' interest but honor their humanity, center their knowledge, and value their voices.

Step 2: Find Relevant Digital Source Material

Today's internet contains a wealth of online curricular ideas, source materials, and virtual networks for English teachers looking to restory digital curriculum in order to decenter whiteness in their classrooms. Many of these digital resources have been created with, by, or for teachers for the purposes of disrupting literary whiteness. For instance, chapter two details #DisruptTexts, a platform created by four women-of-color educators (Julia Torres, Kim Parker, Lorena Germán, and Tricia Ebarvia), and its four principles. The website contains recommended reading, entries from teachers across the country, and suggestions for disrupting canonical texts, including *To Kill a Mockingbird* (1960) and *The Great Gatsby* (1925).

Another resource for restorying digital YA curriculum is the #Wakanda syllabus (initially posted on the shuttered platform Storify) created by Walter Greason (2016). The syllabus provides a list of readings that help viewers to more fully understand the major themes in Marvel's film *Black Panther* (Coogler, 2018) as well as the preceding comics. The readings "provide an opportunity for global audiences to study the traditions of Black nationalism, Pan-Africanism, and the variety of African indigenous cultures" as well as themes of Black fantasy and Afrofuturism. Similarly, the #Lemonade syllabus (2016), created by Candice Benbow, is a collection of works that introduces readers to the written works of Black women that mirror the themes found in Beyoncé's 2016 film *Lemonade* (see Figure 4.2). The syllabus includes the work of Black feminists as well as photography, music, theater, and film. Finally, *#OwnVoices* is a term coined by Corinne Duyvis to highlight authors from historically marginalized groups writing about their own experiences from their own perspectives. Educators will often use the hashtag on Twitter, Facebook, and Instagram to find books written by *and* about people of color.

While this list is by no means exhaustive, it is meant to provide resources for source material that honors topics relevant to the lives of students.

Step 3: Determine a Digital Platform and Engage in Discussions about Critical Media Literacy

Much of the work youth do to restory their own learning outside the walls of the classroom takes place on varied platforms they identify as suitable for their *own* purposes (Griffin, 2021). To that end, when teachers incorporate digital learning into the classroom, they should consider platforms that youth already engage regularly as well as platforms that allow them to learn new skills (we discuss platform authenticity in greater detail in chapter five). For instance, teens have recently taken up the platform TikTok as a place to teach others and to critique the world around them. Likewise, Kelly (2018) explored how Black girls use Snapchat to develop critical resistance in schools. Below, Josh details how Wattpad can be a classroom tool for young people to share their lived realities with a wide audience of digital YAL consumers, experts, and fans.

FIGURE 4.2. The Lemonade Syllabus by Candice Benbow.

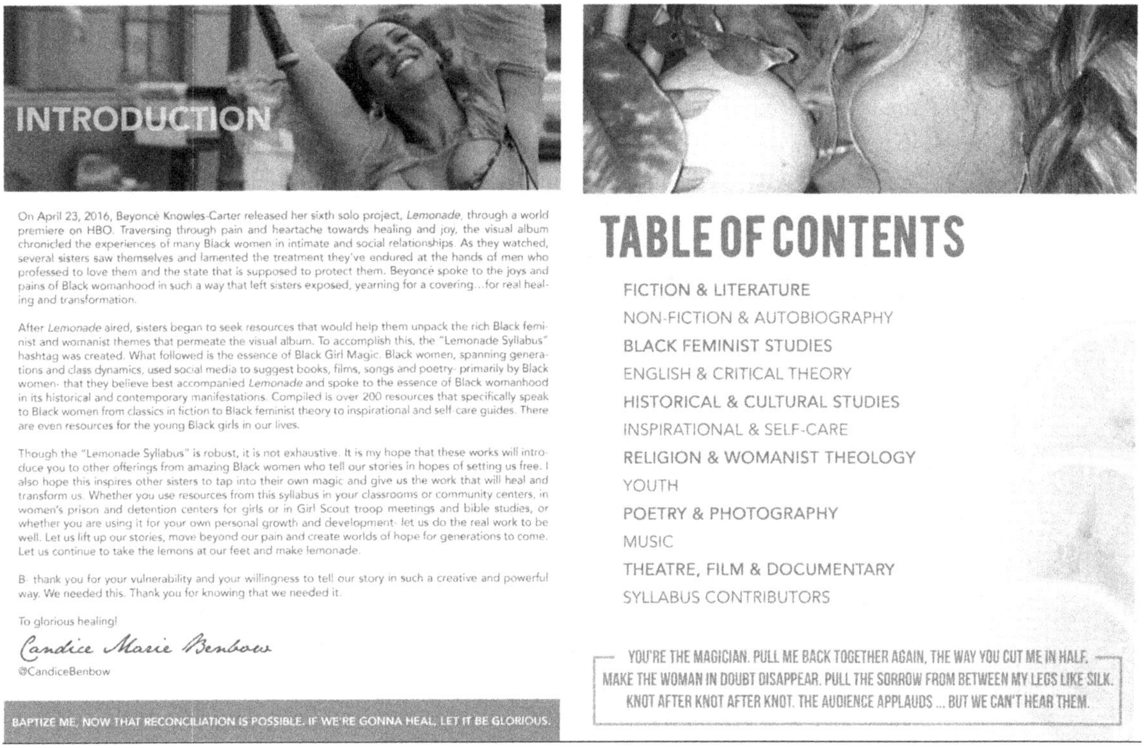

INTRODUCTION

On April 23, 2016, Beyoncé Knowles-Carter released her sixth solo project, *Lemonade*, through a world premiere on HBO. Traversing through pain and heartache towards healing and joy, the visual album chronicled the experiences of many Black women in intimate and social relationships. As they watched, several sisters saw themselves and lamented the treatment they've endured at the hands of men who professed to love them and the state that is supposed to protect them. Beyoncé spoke to the joys and pains of Black womanhood in such a way that left sisters exposed, yearning for a covering…for real healing and transformation.

After *Lemonade* aired, sisters began to seek resources that would help them unpack the rich Black feminist and womanist themes that permeate the visual album. To accomplish this, the "Lemonade Syllabus" hashtag was created. What followed is the essence of Black Girl Magic. Black women, spanning generations and class dynamics, used social media to suggest books, films, songs and poetry- primarily by Black women- that they believe best accompanied *Lemonade* and spoke to the essence of Black womanhood in its historical and contemporary manifestations. Compiled is over 200 resources that specifically speak to Black women from classics in fiction to Black feminist theory to inspirational and self-care guides. There are even resources for the young Black girls in our lives.

Though the "Lemonade Syllabus" is robust, it is not exhaustive. It is my hope that these works will introduce you to other offerings from amazing Black women who tell our stories in hopes of setting us free. I also hope this inspires other sisters to tap into their own magic and give us the work that will heal and transform us. Whether you use resources from this syllabus in your classrooms or community centers, in women's prison and detention centers for girls or in Girl Scout troop meetings and bible studies, or whether you are using it for your own personal growth and development- let us do the real work to be well. Let us lift up our stories, move beyond our pain and create worlds of hope for generations to come. Let us continue to take the lemons at our feet and make lemonade.

B- thank you for your vulnerability and your willingness to tell our story in such a creative and powerful way. We needed this. Thank you for knowing that we needed it.

To glorious healing!

Candice Marie Benbow

@CandiceBenbow

BAPTIZE ME, NOW THAT RECONCILIATION IS POSSIBLE. IF WE'RE GONNA HEAL, LET IT BE GLORIOUS.

TABLE OF CONTENTS

FICTION & LITERATURE
NON-FICTION & AUTOBIOGRAPHY
BLACK FEMINIST STUDIES
ENGLISH & CRITICAL THEORY
HISTORICAL & CULTURAL STUDIES
INSPIRATIONAL & SELF-CARE
RELIGION & WOMANIST THEOLOGY
YOUTH
POETRY & PHOTOGRAPHY
MUSIC
THEATRE, FILM & DOCUMENTARY
SYLLABUS CONTRIBUTORS

YOU'RE THE MAGICIAN. PULL ME BACK TOGETHER AGAIN, THE WAY YOU CUT ME IN HALF. MAKE THE WOMAN IN DOUBT DISAPPEAR. PULL THE SORROW FROM BETWEEN MY LEGS LIKE SILK. KNOT AFTER KNOT AFTER KNOT. THE AUDIENCE APPLAUDS ... BUT WE CAN'T HEAR THEM.

Step 4: Allow Students to Lead the Discussion

Restorying digital YAL calls for reconsideration not only of text and modality but also of pedagogy. Historically, English education succumbed to the banking model of education (Freire, 1970) that required students to memorize a set of rules and regulations regarding reading and writing. Contemporarily, the trend has been for teachers to guide students in discussion about texts and topics *they* (teachers) deem important, providing little opportunity for students to experiment with their own ideas. Above, Autumn explained how she allowed students to guide the conversation by posing their own questions and then using those questions to promote digital discussion. Digital platforms such as Padlet, Wattpad, and Flipgrid allow students the opportunity to engage in digital discourse with their peers with little to no teacher mediation. In engaging discourse in this way, students are able to develop their critical consciousness and practice student leadership, taking on topics that are important to *them* both within and beyond the walls of the school.

Returning to Autumn's Example

Once Autumn's students watched the videos and curated a list of discussion questions, they used their own prompts to guide them through a rich discussion of digital YA culture, racialized messages about skin tone and colorism, and popular culture. The girls drew on their knowledge of history—from Black Creoles in New Orleans in the 1800s to the love triangle of The Notorious B.I.G, Lil' Kim, and Faith Evans in the 1990s—to analyze the ways media messages impact perceptions of skin tone amongst Black folks. Because the topic, source material, and digital platforms not only aligned with their interests but drew on their racialized knowledge and experiences, they were able to engage in discourse that facilitated opportunities to create new knowledge together.

In order to see another example of how another teacher worked with students to cultivate a digital YAL curriculum, we now turn to an example from digital YAL fandom.

Section 2: Un-Whitewashing Fandom: Becoming a Fan of Digital YAL

As we laid out in the first section of this chapter, humanities curricula have historically been white property. ELA curricula, as one form of those curricula, have continually demonstrated commitments to white supremacy through the preservation of canon. There are, however, powerful alternatives to that white canon, and fandom is one of the most promising that embraces digital YAL and digital YA culture. As Henry Jenkins (2013) explains in describing fandom, "There are, of course, many different types of fans—rock fans, sports fans, movie buffs, opera enthusiasts, etc." (p. 1). As teachers, we are likely fans too, whether of particular curricular approaches, pedagogical tools, or, of course, YAL. Jenkins continues his description of fans by revealing how individual fans form into distinct cultures or "fandoms" that are created and maintained online. Media fandoms, in particular, have sometimes "fan-atic" followings that carry within them the capacity to reinforce or reform white, straight, cisgender, ableist norms within canon.

Harry Potter fandom, for example, has reformed such norms by restorying the world and its characters. Specifically, Harry Potter and the books' author have been taken to task for its commitments to whiteness and colonialization as well as author Rowling's vehement antitrans stance (Dahlen & Thomas, 2022). Fans, however, have found ways to reimagine the source material toward more critical orientations, through fandom and digital texts. Fans restoried the world, writing in Black, queer, trans, and disabled characters to challenge the "canon." Distinct from the literary canon broadly, "canon" in fandom refers to the original story world created by an author, and fans rewrite that world, filling it with more just representation. For instance, in "What Story, What Identity, Wattpad?" (Coleman and Hall, 2019), Josh explored how queer and trans youth used Wattpad, a digital platform, to restory dominant narratives of white, cis-heteronormativity in queer media, specifically in the blockbuster hit *Love, Simon*. He spotlighted "bending" practices, in which young fans restoried identity within the text. These young people used "racebending" and "genderbending" to create new narratives in which the protagonist's whiteness and cisgender identity were reimagined. They created the representations they needed to see in the world.

Of significance, teachers can invite fans, fandoms, and fan practices into their classroom to restory humanities and English curricula as white property. Easier said than done, including fandom in your classroom can be quite challenging. As the previous paragraph demonstrates, there is a great deal of domain-specific vocabulary—*fan, fandom, canon,* and *bending* to name just a few—and this vocabulary can be isolating for students and teachers. (See Table 4.2 for a definition of these terms.) Moreover, fandom has historically been stigmatized due to its connection to (fan)tasy and genres of speculative fiction. Addressing these concerns in the remainder of this section, Josh provides five steps for integrating fandom into classrooms in order to un-whitewash ELA curriculum.

Step 1: Stop the Stigma

What comes to mind when you think of the word *fan* or *fangirl*? Perhaps you think immediately of Rainbow Rowell's hit YA novel of the same name. More often, however, the term *fangirl* summons a reductive image of a white adolescent who obsesses—dare we say, fanatically—over some teenage heartthrob. Unfortunately, this understanding of fans shapes how fandom is understood both in the general population and in schools. Often, folks think the reading and writing that occurs on fandoms is unsophisticated, emotional outpourings by lachrymose teens. Notably, such ideas of fandom rest on white, colonial, and misogynistic norms that hold emotions and reason separate. For the classroom, this informs the misconception that good writing is measured writing, objective writing. It fails to explore the reason for emotions and the ways in which emotions can inform impassioned writing.

Fandom, by contrast, is a space that embraces impassioned writing. It invites readers and writers to geek out! And it invites them to share their passions with the world—doing so in ways that challenge reductive images of fandom as all-white, all-straight, all-cis, and all-women. It might, however, take some finagling to get students onboard. In his English education classes, Josh shares how he is an aca-fan (academic who is also a fan) when teaching about restorying. He shares his past love of Harry Potter (HP) and current conflict with the series as well as his love of *Avatar: The Last Airbender* (2005). He also asks students if anyone is a fan or participates in fandom in order to activate prior knowledge and locate potential leaders for future writers' workshops. Being vulnerable about your own fannish ways can invite students to be vulnerable in return while establishing a culture in which fan writers are safe and respected. Furthermore, there are almost always a couple of fandom experts in a class. Positioning them as knowers, experts, and quite practically group leaders can help students navigate the platforms and norms of fandom. The last key is to help your students locate their own fandoms, particularly in connection to digital YAL. It's important to understand that fandoms are repositories of digital YAL as well as spaces in which digital YA culture is forged and sustained, and locating the right fandom online can provide students with a community and culture in which to embrace their inner fan while striving toward more just representation.

Step 2: Teach the Terms

Like with any new text or technology, one of the first tasks to integrating fandom into your classroom is providing students with the vocabulary and conceptual knowledge necessary to access it. Typical prereading strategies work well here, and teachers can build a bridge between what students already know about fandom and the writing skills demanded by teaching strategies. To ensure students are set up to write critically online, let's first go over some crucial vocabulary.

In their Vox.com article "Canon, Fanon, Shipping and More" (2016), Aja Romano (they/she) provides a brief explanation of fandom as well as definitions of some key terms related to it. While their article's array of vocabulary is quite exhaustive, we have curated several introductory lists that can help students "Get Involved," "Get Going," and "Get Critical" with fandom (see Tables 4.2–4.4).

TABLE 4.2. List of introductory terms.

"Get Involved"		
Term	**Definition**	**Example**
Fandom	A community of fans	Harry Potter (HP) Fandom
Canon	The source material	HP novels
Fannish	An adjective describing something related to fandom	"Having a HP themed classroom! How fannish."
Fanfiction or Fanfic	Fiction written about a previously existing work	HP fanfic is everywhere online.
Fanworks	Creations you base on canon	Fan art, fan vids, cosplay, fan comics, fan films, podfics, etc.

TABLE 4.3. List of mainstream digital fandoms.

"Get Going"		
Name	**Description**	**URL**
FF.net	Short for fanfiction.net. This online community has existed since 1998 and is one of the most popular multi-fandom fanfiction archives on the internet.	Fanfiction.net
Wattpad	Online self-publishing platform that has dwarfed many other fanfiction archives. This platform, which has an extremely popular app, skews younger and often focuses on celebrity fandoms.	Wattpad.com
AO3	The Archive of Our Own is the largest entirely fan-run, noncorporate fanfiction archive on the internet. It is an offshoot by fans from LiveJournal.	Archiveofourown.org
AsianFanFics	An Asian/Asian American–focused fan community that publishes content about, for, and by Asian/Asian Americans.	Asisanfanfics.com

TABLE 4.4. List of Terms to Promote Critical Inquiry

"Get Critical"		
Term	**Definition**	**Example**
AU or Alternative Universe	Alternative Universe is a type of fanfic in which canonical characters are placed into a different setting, universe, or timeline. This is also how students restory time.	Place HP in a world in which Germany won World War II
Genderbending	Genderbent fic is fic that changes the gender of one or more of the canonical characters.	Rewrite HP as a trans character.
Racebending	The act of changing a canonical character's race. While originally this term was used to call out whitewashing in Hollywood, it can now refer to restoried writings that un-whitewash digital YAL and media.	Rewriting Harry Potter as if he were Indian American.
Queerbaiting	Writing storylines that exploit queer fans by teasing them for ratings without any intention of making characters canonically or fanonically queer.	Implying Harry Potter is pansexual, though never naming it.

Step 3: Dive into Digital Fandom

The next step for integrating digital fandom into your classroom is to dive in online! Students need to learn by exploring fandoms for themselves; however, they should do this with guidance. Be explicit with your students that digital YA fandom can be overwhelming on your first go. In Josh's young adult literature class, he asks pre- and inservice ELA teachers to read Ebony Elizabeth Thomas and Amy Stornaiuolo's (2016) article "Restorying the Self," and then in class, he invites them to become Digital Detectives (see chapter three for the description of this activity) and dive into fandom. Having done this for several years, he can verify that it is always met with mixed responses. For some, it is overwhelming. The terms, platform, cultural norms, and sheer quantity of digital YAL leads some educators to feel quite dazed. For others, fandom's digital YA culture is exciting and full of possibility. However, these folks tend to be in the minority. Accordingly, through trial and error, Josh has learned a couple of necessary steps for introducing students to fandom.

First, name the potential for discomforting feelings to arise. Share with students that their first experiences of fandom might be uncomfortable, especially if they are cultural outsiders to the online community. Instruct them that it's okay to wade into the messiness and know you will learn together through the journey. Next, chunk the experience for students by modeling how to navigate both fandom and the digital platform you believe is best for your class. Josh recommends beginning with Wattpad. It's user-friendly, oriented toward younger audiences, and is easily accessible via web browser or app. Teachers might then focus on reading digital YAL in class to illuminate how fandom rewrites canon.

For instance, if you have read *The Hate U Give* by Angie Thomas (2017) in your class, you might model and think aloud what you notice as you type *The Hate U Give* into the search bar on Wattpad.com. Next, explain how you choose a story from the list provided. Be sure to explain that the eye icon next to a story indicates views and the star icon indicates likes, and these help you know which stories have been most vetted and enjoyed by a wide array of members of the fandom. From there, invite students to read silently for a bit. Once they have read a "chapter" or so of the story (these are often quite short in fandom), then ask students to practice using the vocabulary words provided in step 2, while discussing the follow questions:

- What was it like navigating this fandom?
- How did this fanfic alter "canon" from the novel?
- What did you notice about the "inline comments" on the fanwork?
- What do you notice about the writing?
- What are some drawbacks or concerns you have about fandom?

Next, invite students to explore Wattpad on their own and search through the stories of a particular fandom they are interested in (e.g., Harry Potter, *Avatar: The Last Airbender*, etc.). Moreover, they should take notice of the ways in which the curriculum is restoried in terms of race, gender, sexuality, and more. One way to do this is by searching for tags within stories, such as "racebending," "genderbending," "police abolition," etc. Finally, allow students to have an additional debriefing session in their groups using the same questions as before. Once students have done this, it's time for them to begin writing fanfic of their own.

A Caution: Fandom can be a sexy place. Scholars have documented the ways in which queer communities, feminist communities, and more have used fandom to explore their own sexualities, to imagine who they are within and across digital YAL fandoms (Coleman, 2019, Coleman & Hall, 2019; Jenkins, 2012). For some users, whether queer, straight, or questioning, fandom has provided a safe place to reimagine themselves by writing sexually explicit material. Accordingly, the term or tag PWP—"Plot? What plot?" or "porn without plot"—has been used to mark this content. With this in mind, it's important to build students' critical media literacy skills and self-awareness to know if accessing these texts is appropriate. The NCTE "Report of the Task Force on Critical Media Literacy" can provide resources and suggestions for building these skills (https://tinyurl.com/NCTECriticalMediaLiteracy).

Step 4: Begin with Bending

Now that you've modeled exploring fandom, it's time to invite students to think, imagine, and write like a fan. As explained in the introduction to this book, restorying is a theory and writing practice generated from fan communities. This means that each of the six forms of restorying—identity, place, mode, perspective, metanarrative, and time—were derived from what fans were already writing online. While some students in your class might be ready to write online, we recommend using writers' workshops to guide students through the writing process. Specifically, ELA teachers might name the rhetorical situation as writing restoried fanfiction for a fandom of students' choosing. Fortunately for teaching, fan writing aligns nicely with tried-and-true methods of writing pedagogy and, particularly, with creative writing–oriented writers' workshops. Furthermore, naming fandom as your students' intended audience invites critical writing that can challenge ELA curricula as white property when aligned with restorying practices.

As Josh recommends in his Wattpad article, when inviting students to write restoried fanfic, "begin with bending" (Coleman and Hall, 2019, p. 66). Restorying identity through racebending, genderbending, queerbending, classbending, or even speciesbending (Coleman, 2022) invites wild imaginings into students' writing processes, and it is also easily tailored toward critical approaches to reading and writing. For instance, teachers can invite their students to reimagine the protagonist of a class novel or even one of their favorite pieces of YAL or media by bending the race, gender, or sexuality of their identity.

Suggested Prompts

Prompt 1: Based upon one of your own identities that is different from that of the protagonist's in our class text, write a reimagined synopsis of the plot. Remember that restorying identity requires more than simply exchanging one identity for another; it demands that the plot be fundamentally altered. For instance, a romance about a straight, white cisgender protagonist would occur quite differently if the protagonist were instead a trans, queer person of color, yet all other characters and setting remained the same.

Prompt 2: Draw upon your lived experiences to restory the identity of one of your favorite young adult novel, show, or movie protagonists, and write a synopsis of the text. Remember that restorying identity requires more than simply exchanging one identity for another; it demands that the plot be fundamentally altered. For instance, a romance about a straight, white cisgender protagonist would occur quite differently if the protagonist were instead a trans, queer person of color, yet all other characters remained the same.

Engaging Ethics: It's important to understand that the work of reimagining race, gender, and sexuality can open many critical conversations that teachers might facilitate. However, it also raises some ethical considerations. At first, students should shy away from writing experiences that do not mirror their own, especially without thorough research. This can result in stereotypes and misrepresentations that are damaging to historically marginalized communities. It's best to bend from one's own unique experiences, at least initially.

Restorying identity requires imagination, writerly persistence, and a bit of reckless abandon. For their first forays into restorying, students should be encouraged to draw from their lived experiences, particularly when brainstorming and drafting their restory. Engaged in writers' workshop, they might then consult with their peers and with you, their teacher, to test out their speculative ideas. Once students have generated a synopsis that fundamentally reconfigures "canon," students might then craft a "key scene" from the text into fanfic that foregrounds the protagonist's restoried identity.

Step 5: Publish Your Product

The final step for students to challenge white "canon" is to publish their work. This can be done within the class through a gallery walk or a digital repository, or for those who are ready, they can post their "key scene" or fanfic to Wattpad. Students need to think carefully about the tags they use to describe their story as this will invite particular communities within fandom to read their work. Lastly, prepare students to engage with commenters. While Wattpad tends to be a generally kind and supportive community, trolls are always lurking. Warn your students that some negative commentary may occur, but with the right disposition, we can decide what is constructive and helpful versus what is simply mean. Again, these are all critical media literacy skills that have become part and parcel of our twenty-first century digital era.

Conclusion

Throughout this chapter, we—Josh, Autumn, and Ebony—provided examples for how to un-whitewash literacy curricula by using digital YAL and digital YA culture to facilitate spaces where students can actively contribute as knowledge makers during the planning process as well as restory literary canon by engaging in digital fandom communities. We've outlined the varied mindsets, practices of reflection, and ethical considerations necessary to engage students in this type of online learning, and it is our hope that teachers willfully take up the challenge of disrupting notions of literacy curricula as white property. As mentioned above, our ever-growing digital world requires new methods of teaching and engaging, especially as adolescents grow to spend more and more of their waking hours online.

While we acknowledge the task of keeping up with new platforms and ways of communicating has its challenges, we believe when we partner with students and allow their digital interests, knowledges, and skills to guide classroom discourse, we are better able to facilitate learning that disrupts homogenized literacy curricula and opens up possibilities for students' present and future lives—possibilities that are not limited by the four walls of the classroom. Extending this work, in chapter five, "Restorying Multimodality," we explore the expanded modality of digital YAL made possible by digital technologies. Specifically, we spotlight how young people engage in narrative production, both with and without teacher support, and the chapter concludes by advancing pedagogical approaches for embracing youth-crafted digital YA productions (e.g., personal youth narratives) that harness a fuller range of young people's online and in-person networks.

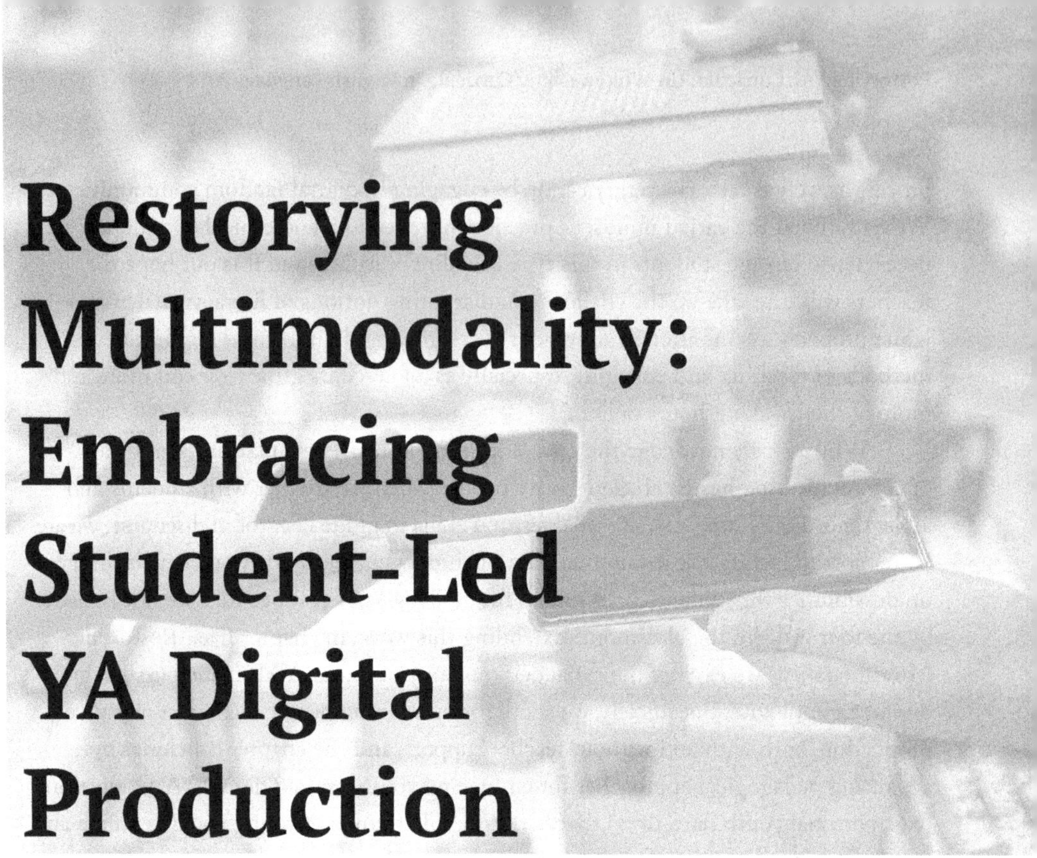

Chapter Five

Restorying Multimodality: Embracing Student-Led YA Digital Production

In a world that is becoming more digital by the day—especially in the age of COVID-19—educators are relying more heavily on digital tools and platforms to create spaces that facilitate learning. As noted in earlier chapters, digital YAL provides readers space for creative, imaginative, disruptive, and critical work to take place. Engaging in digital YA culture by taking up multimodal tools creates opportunities for students to partake in the work of identity development. However, the digital is not a panacea, and the digital alone will not save us. In fact, employing digital tools in the classroom requires perhaps even more thoughtfulness, as teachers wade through the myriad of options for platforms and modalities they might use and *how* they might use them. Connected to recommendation four of this book's guiding position statement, the digital is demanding new considerations of "us[ing] appropriate pedagogy" for inviting students to engage critically with digital YAL and digital YA culture (*Preparing Teachers*, 2018).

Research has suggested that although teachers write digital learning into curriculum, it can sometimes become a continuation of the rote learning that takes place in classrooms, essentially moving worksheets and novels from paper to the screen (Griffin, 2021). When this happens, there is no platform, no website, and no digital tool that will inherently create a more just educational system. Often, students form their own online communities away from teachers and adults, and these young people are expert navigators of those online spaces. Thus, teachers don't have to—and likely should not—have a hand in all of the work young people do. Instead, we argue that teachers might invite students to take the lead in their own learning and production as they navigate the digital platforms and multimodal tools most natural to them. Doing so not only places agency back in their hands, but it also allows for much richer learning experiences as students are able to draw on their funds of knowledge (Moll, 2019).

Below, we present work from two studies of student-led digital YA production—the product of youth-authored digital texts—as a way of modeling what might be done in classrooms and the third spaces beyond them. For each study, we provide a road map for teachers interested in learning to expand uses of the digital in their classroom and to spotlight the educational potential of allowing young people to drive the production of digital YA into the future. Specifically, we highlight how teachers need to advocate, as the NCTE position statement states, for "freedom and autonomy" (*Preparing Teachers*, 2018), not merely for their own teaching and learning but for students to craft and share their own narratives with the world.

In the first example, contributing author Bethany Monea, a literacy researcher and educator, and her collaborating youth researchers Perla Gonzalez, Joselyn Andrade, and Keiry Chicas, three undergraduate media makers, share their collective decision to create their YouTube channel, LatiNXT GEN, and purvey three vignettes about their experiences with digital production. The channel, as well as the vignettes below, details the students' transition from high school into their first year of college and highlights their racialized and gendered experiences as well as how their first year of college was impacted by the COVID-19 pandemic. In the second example, contributing author Rabani Garg, also a literacy researcher, shares her experiences working with youth whose digital writings are deeply informed by their digital networks and discourse. The section explores her work with five adolescent boys in New Delhi, India, providing a global perspective on digital YA production, and it focuses on the YA digital production of student author Shyamu Korwa.

Section 1: Engaging YouTube to Tell Our Stories

Bethany Monea, PhD candidate, University of Pennsylvania
Perla Gonzalez, Joselyn Andrade, and Keiry Chicas, student authors

Throughout section 1 of this chapter, "we" refers to Bethany, Perla, Joselyn, and Keiry, and together we offer teacher-readers our experiences producing digital YA stories online that disrupt dominant narratives within digital YA culture. As an authorship team comprising a literacy researcher/educator (Bethany) and three undergraduate media makers (Joseyln, Perla, and Keiry), we encourage English teachers to help their students develop critical and creative capacities that contribute to digital YA culture through the analysis and production of digital YA narratives. We argue that, in turn, this creates opportunities for all students to tell their own stories in their own ways, both within the classroom and beyond. As a non-Latinx white researcher and three students of color committed to antiracist pedagogies, we emphasize the importance of storytelling because "it allows us to put our collective stories in conversation with one another and against dominant narratives and stories that perpetuate white privilege, white supremacy, and patriarchy" (Johnson et al., 2017, p. 470). To do this, we draw on Keiry's, Joselyn's, and Perla's experiences as authors of digital young adult stories who have been engaged in a long-term research and filmmaking project with Bethany and several other Latinx students. In this project, we tell stories on YouTube about college transitions that disrupt dominant, white-centric narratives about going to college. We tell these stories of our own different experiences as digital content creators to offer suggestions for educators who want to (1) help students develop critical media literacy, (2) develop students' multimodal literacies, through which they can author their own stories within and beyond the classroom, and (3) teach students to use critical digital composing to disrupt the dominant and monolithic narratives that circulate throughout digital YA culture and school curricula.

Context

The four of us came together to write this section as members of a long-term, ongoing participatory research project, which Bethany began facilitating as part of her graduate studies. Before beginning this work together, we all knew of each other's existence in some way thanks to a college-readiness program for first-generation students in which Perla, Joselyn, and Keiry had been enrolled since eighth grade. Bethany, who had begun volunteering with the program as a writing tutor, reached out to twelfth-grade students to ask if they wanted to join a research project investigating "through filmmaking" the transition to college. Joselyn, Perla, and Keiry, along with several other students, signed up for the project, and it didn't take long for all of us to get close and bond.

Little did we know how hectic the students' senior year and first year of college would be, as we (Joseyln, Keiry, and Perla) graduated high school and began college in 2020 during the COVID-19 pandemic. As first-generation Latinx students, we were the first in our families to go to college; we were all excited, but we did not expect it was going to require an extra push of perseverance to overcome the virtual barrier. Not only did our scholastic lives shift into the digital sphere, but our social lives did as well. As we moved aspects of our lives online, it was even more important for us to become critical consumers of screen-based media and more knowledgeable about the platforms through which we were consuming it, including how white- and male-centric narratives dominated the digital landscape.

As a research and filmmaking team, we worked together on various projects. We began by publishing YouTube videos on a channel we created called LatiNXT GEN in which we introduced ourselves to the world and created episodes that told stories about our individual and collective journeys from high school to college, such as how COVID-19 disrupted our senior year of high school, how we began college online, and how we navigated difficult decisions about college. As time moved forward, so did this research, and we have still been able to give guest lectures for other students and preservice teachers as well as attend academic conferences, where we present ourselves to other individuals who are conducting similar research or have interest in our work. We have also engaged in group discussions, collaborative analysis, and writing sessions in which we've discussed dominant narratives, and we've developed lesson plans teachers can use to have similar conversations with their students, as we share at the end of this section.

At the time of this writing, Keiry, Perla, and Joselyn are rising sophomores and Bethany is completing her PhD. We have learned many things, and we share our experiences with one another and with the other Latinx first-gen students with whom we make videos—nine different perspectives on one simple thing: college. But one thing for sure we all mutually agree on is everyone's experience is different, and college is possible; you just got to keep on moving forward. We hope teachers share our stories with their first-generation students to allow them to realize that higher education is possible. Our stories are available at https://tinyurl.com/LatiNXTGEN.

Our Experiences with Digital Narrative Production

Throughout our work together, we have come to realize and reiterate the importance of centering our own stories and embracing their differences. In that spirit, we share the collective story of our decision to create a YouTube channel and offer three narrative vignettes to highlight the process of Joselyn's, Keiry's, and Perla's experiences with digital production. Our aim in this chapter is to share the story of this process with English teachers who can draw inspiration from our productions to foster the critical analysis and production of digital YA culture within their own classrooms.

When LatiNXT GEN was in its early stages of development, our group discussed multiple aspects of the project (including audience, how we would collaborate, our mission, our identities, etc.) in order to better guide us in how we would choose to share our stories. One matter of importance in choosing a platform was finding one that would allow us to create media that was representative of both interconnected and independent narratives and identities amongst the members in our group. Therefore, we needed a platform that was accessible when we wanted to publish collaborative work as well as when we wanted to publish individual work from amongst the group so every person would be able to create media that gave their story justice. In addition to this, there was a strong emphasis on choosing a platform that was accessible to our wide-ranging audience. We wanted our work to benefit both youth and educators. Through our videos, future and current educators can get to know their students and connect with them on a deeper level. We do not want our work to simply be digital YA stories put out in the world to no effect; we want our stories to encourage action within classroom settings. So, we chose to create a YouTube channel—LatiNXT GEN—because it fulfilled these goals, enabling us to upload both collaboratively and individually created episodes onto a channel we could easily share with others.

These stories demonstrate the criticality with which we engaged with the dominant narratives about college transition that circulate on YouTube and the creativity with which we produced our own stories for this platform. As a group, we have discussed some of the dominant narratives we hope our YouTube series disrupts, such as:

- "College pathways have a clear and predictable structure."
- "College is the time to find ourselves."
- "You got accepted into college because of affirmative action."
- "Community college is not good . . . you have to go to a four-year college straight off the bat."
- The normalization of unhealthy, toxic competition amongst students.

Our videos emphasize both our similarities and our differences as first-gen and Latinx students, allowing us to disrupt narratives associated with these identities, such as the ones listed above. Collaborative storytelling let us explore general themes we shared, but individual narratives (like the ones described below) helped us to disrupt monolithic representations of minoritized students. Ultimately, we aimed to show how—even though we are often placed under the same labels—we each have different stories and paths we take throughout college and our lives.

Telling our own stories in our own way on YouTube helped us realize that even though we (Perla, Joselyn, Keiry, and our collaborators) are all first-gen and all Latinx, we have different stories to share, and the differences in our stories counter both the dominant narratives about going to college and the monolithic representations of first-gen and minoritized students. Although youth participants in this study all identify as Latinx, our families have different immigration histories, impacting how we understand Latinidad. In addition, our first-gen and Latinx identities intersect with other aspects of our identities (e.g., gender, sexuality, socioeconomic status) in different ways, resulting in different lenses, interpretations, and significance. Sharing these stories on YouTube (in contrast to sharing them in an essay for a class, for example) has allowed us to reach a larger audience, including other students who can relate to our stories. The process of digital YA production also allowed us as individuals to regain power over our narratives because we can make our own artistic choices for how and when we present our stories, as we describe below.

Quote from Keiry's Video

"I decided for one month, this month of October, to record and see how much I can change myself both physically and mentally. By the end of the month of October, my goal was to become a butterfly, you know, to be beautiful and bold and be a better version of myself or at least to become a better version of myself."

Screenshot from Keiry's Video

"I'm always studying, doing work . . ."

Keiry

I chose to tell my story on this platform because the world is changing; everything is slowly becoming virtual. Upcoming generations will come to see my story along with my friends' stories about how as first gens, we were able to overcome barriers and were still able to complete our first year, second year, and so on, specifically when these future generations graduate college. Growing up, I have always seen school-related videos on YouTube, such as back-to-school shopping, college appearances, and even specific outfits for school; however, I never saw videos from students who share the same story as mine: Latinx First Gen. I wanted to know more about what college life was like but from someone who went through the same experiences I did. I chose to tell my story on YouTube because that's where all the school-related content I saw growing up was shared. I decided to share an eight-minute thirty-second video to explain my life in a month of college. A big central idea of that video was comparing my life to the life of a butterfly—how it transforms from a caterpillar to a beautiful creature. I focused on being a caterpillar at the beginning of the month of October and being a transformed butterfly at the end of the month. Even though I didn't complete the goals I set for myself, I was still able to learn more about myself and become that butterfly. In the video, I didn't just include the educational aspect, but I also chose to portray my entire life and be vulnerable. Putting this video out to the public allows other Latinx First Gens who happen to scroll through YouTube begin to binge on different type of back-to-school videos than the ones I did.

Perla

I chose to tell my story on YouTube because it's something all people my age use and watch, day in and day out. The video I made for our YouTube series was a four-minute thirty-second video to explain what happened to my college decision due of the pandemic. The story in my video is about how I was not going to the four-year college I had originally chosen and was instead going to a community college. I chose to tell this story because it's something that isn't really spoken about or seen much, especially when it came to the students at the high school I attended, where the majority were not first-gen students and were predominantly white. Toward the end of my senior year, everyone was going to a four-year college, so I felt the need to do the same—if I went to the community college, there would be a lot of stigma associated with it. In order to tell my story, I chose to do a day-in-the-life video about what it was like living at home, having a job, and going to school full time by telling my story of changing my plans to attend community college. I believe making a story time video doesn't always have to be someone sitting in front of a camera and speaking directly to it. Instead, I chose to make a video that was trending with other popular YouTube videos, a day-in-my-life video, and combine it with narration. YouTube made producing and sharing my video easy. My subject was something that attracts teenagers like me but shows a different aspect of college and what it's like for me.

Quote from Perla's Video

"But now I am at NOVA, I am a teacher education major, I have a job with my best friend, and might be getting another job soon, I have my best friends around me, and I am healthy and safe at home. And that two years down the road I will be transferring to another college, and I will still get that same college experience there."

Screenshot from Perla's Video

"This was a very difficult decision . . ."

Joselyn

When we had our group discussions regarding what platform would work best for both us as the creators and for our targeted audience, I resonated with a majority of our areas of concerns and our focuses. While the decision to use YouTube was a collaborative decision, the decision as to what kind of content we would put on our channel was more intricate, especially regarding the individual stories. I had to do a lot of self-reflection about which stories I was willing to share and which ones I was not. Having these conversations with myself was difficult; as much as I wanted to share personal stories and forward our group's goals, I made the choice to not do so right away in order to protect myself. There's a lot of vulnerability that goes into sharing personal stories online, especially on a popular platform like YouTube. I needed to be mindful. My narratives are my own, and I have the right to tell them any time and any way I desire without any obligation to anyone. Dismantling narratives can be done in a healthy manner in which it's not done at the expense of myself or others. I found that becoming mindful of the stories I was ready to share allowed the message behind my individual

Quote from Joselyn's Video

"My academic insecurity tells me to continue cosmetology, but I want to dedicate my time towards college. After all, the idea of going to college was a dream instilled within me since kindergarten and, well, cosmetology is still very much recent. I'm still undecided about my decision for the future, and that's okay."

Screenshot from Joselyn's Video

"My desire of continuing cosmetology collided with my dream of going to college."

videos become stronger. For example, one video I did was about me debating whether or not to continue my cosmetology profession during my time in college. By giving myself time to reflect on that situation, I was able to tell my story holistically, given where my thoughts were at the time. I had a clear vision of how I wanted the video to look, so the making and editing of it was quite peaceful. I strongly believe if I had chosen to share that story prematurely, the message and how it was conveyed within the video would have been lost and, in a way, incomplete. Using YouTube as our platform allowed for me to take time and develop my stories to the extent that I felt comfortable sharing them.

We are hoping these digital YA stories of our personal experiences can inspire English teachers to break the mold of dominant narratives and modalities by facilitating space for students to tell their own stories, in their own ways, in their own time, and on platforms that are important and accessible to them. We want teachers who read this to engage "appropriate pedagogy" (Buehler et al., 2018, p. 4) that encourages their students to express themselves through different platforms and media rather than only through products that fit traditional, dominant understandings of what storytelling and English curricula might look like (e.g., written essays). By doing so, teachers will cultivate an open and welcoming environment for personal reflection, allowing students to engage creativity and mindfulness while doing their assignments. In support of this goal, we offer a lesson development guide we developed for teachers to use and modify. This two-part guide can be used in a classroom setting to help students understand dominant narratives while the students are also given the opportunity to express themselves in different modalities.

Lesson Development Guide

Guiding Question

How can teachers support students in the critical analysis and production of digital YA stories?

Suggested Prework: Since one's own identity and its intersectional components (e.g., gender, ethnicity, race, sexuality, age, geographic location) are central to how one receives and tells stories, we suggest teachers and students engage in personal discovery conversations about their own and others' identities in advance of this lesson.

Suggested Community Agreements and Expectations *We suggest teachers and students establish these together before engaging in discussions about personal narratives.*
• Make sure everyone has a chance to participate and tell their story. • Only tell your story when you are ready. • Respect others' boundaries about what they wish to share. • Take these conversations seriously. • Listen with empathy. *[We suggest teachers and students also work together to create their own agreements unique to their environments.]*

PART ONE: Critical Analysis of Dominant YA Narratives and Platforms
Objectives: Critically analyze dominant YA narratives and develop a better understanding of media literacy in relation to how media perpetuates dominant YA narratives about groups of people.
Step One: *Defining and Identifying Dominant Narratives* In step one, the teacher introduces the concept of dominant narratives by opening the classroom up to discussion on what the students think dominant narratives are. The teacher begins by asking students the question: *What are dominant narratives? Who tells dominant narratives? How do dominant narratives function in our society today?* Within the ongoing discussion, the teacher pauses and introduces a minigame/activity. In this activity, the teacher shares a list of possible dominant narratives (e.g., the competition amongst students is normal and healthy, "money = power," anyone can succeed if they work hard enough), and then the students are asked to sort each one into whether they think it is or isn't a dominant narrative. After they sort narratives based on their dominance, the teacher prompts students to consider the power and problems of dominant narratives with questions such as: • How does this narrative circulate? How does it gain/maintain/sustain power? • Who benefits from the perpetuation of this narrative? Who might be harmed? • When this narrative is dominant, what other narratives are excluded?
Step Two: *The Problems of Dominant Narratives in Our Own Lives* After the teacher has introduced students to what dominant narratives are and how they function, the teacher then shifts the conversation to discuss more personal examples. The teacher asks the students whether or not they believe it is hard for all people to conform to these stereotypical narratives. As the students begin to answer the question, the teacher also asks the students why they think the answer is what they chose. After all the students who would like to engage with the question have done so, the teacher summarizes the themes they heard in the students' responses and provides an example of their own. For example, the teacher could say: "The answer to the question of whether we think dominant narratives are hard for young adults to fit in is it depends on the person. This is because not everyone has the same label or has the same background. An example of this is when I . . . [teacher provides examples of when they did not fit into a dominant narrative of their own]."

Step Three: *Digital Portrayals of Dominant YA Narratives*
In this part of the lesson, the teacher guides students to think about how dominant narratives regarding young adulthood are portrayed online and the role platforms play in circulating them and perpetuating them. If appropriate, the teacher might ask students to log in to their own YouTube or TikTok accounts and compare with each other the types of videos that are "trending" or "suggested" on each other's accounts. The teacher then prompts students to log out of their accounts to see how the "suggested" content changes and asks students: Why do certain digital YA stories get circulated more than others online? The teacher can bring up discussion points such as algorithms, advertising revenue, and sponsored content to help students analyze this question. The teacher should then ask students to consider the advantages and disadvantages of only seeing certain types of digital YA stories online and to consider who benefits when dominant narratives are "trending."

PART TWO: Critical Composing and Restorying Dominant Narratives
Objective: Creatively compose multimodal stories that resist and restory dominant narratives.
Step One: *Reimagining Dominant Narratives* Once students have a better understanding of what dominant narratives are and how they are portrayed online, the teacher once again comes back to the minigame from part one, step one and asks them to disrupt any dominant narratives again based on their discussions. After going through the given examples, the teacher introduces an assignment in which the students are asked what dominant narratives have impacted their lives. After each student has chosen a dominant narrative about their young adulthood, the teacher asks them to consider which aspects of this dominant YA narrative they might reimagine to better fit their own stories, interests, or identities. The teacher might want to use the restorying framework offered by Thomas and Stornaiuolo (2016) to ask students how they might reimagine particular aspects of a dominant narrative such as (1) place, (2) time, (3) mode, (4) perspective, (5) identity, and (6) metanarratives (p. 317). (*Note: Even if a student is part of the dominant identity category portrayed by the dominant narrative, that student can choose a dominant narrative and portray how someone may not fit into that dominant narrative and how that person's life can be impacted by not fitting into it.*)
Step Two: *Restorying Dominant YA Narratives* After the teacher has explained the project in depth and answered any outstanding questions, they can help students choose a media that can best restory or reimagine their selected dominant YA narrative. The teacher might ask: "Why tell this story in this way?" The goal is to get the students to use a different modality other than an essay and to get the students thinking about how someone can tell a story without words. This gives the students the ability to reach out of their comfort zones and to think about how different media types reach different audiences. Not only does it get the students thinking about how media affects narrative portrayal, but it also has them consider how people interpret media differently because of their own experiences.

In the section above, Bethany and her students engaged the digital to restory multimodality, moving across various modes of literacy (print and video). In doing so, they redistributed power and agency amongst the group from a teacher/leader-student dynamic to a cohort of individuals learning alongside one another. In what follows, Rabani furthers this disruption of power, exploring the agency of the digital and its multimodal affordances. She does this by tracing how students leap across platforms, moving effortlessly from the digital to the physical and back again, and they do so across international contexts.

Section 2: Youth Writers in a Networked Literacy Ecosystem

Rabani Garg, PhD candidate, University of Pennsylvania
Shyamu Korwa, student author

Through her work in outside-of-school spaces, Rabani, a literacy researcher and community practitioner, has come to recognize that youth digital YA production, whether in school or out of school, formal or informal, occurs simultaneously across networks, platforms, and modalities. Youth writing engages both local and the more global (wider) networks that young people are a part of. In a long-term writing project with a group of youth[1] in New Delhi, India, Rabani's students have often shared with her that they are not active social media users. However, she noticed they *are* actively engaged digital writers, and they take up ideas and conversations from their various networks (e.g., home, school, community, virtual) in their writings. Their writing moves across multiple interconnected spaces.

Tracing two examples of digital artifacts created in 2020, this section highlights how Shyamu—then in grade 12—draws from local and global networks to create a writing ecosystem that informs the two multimodal artifacts presented here. This section spotlights two key takeaways based on Shyamu's work:

1. Youth writing is situated within an ecosystem that includes multimodal networks that are global and local, in school and out of school, and even at times offline.
2. Young people's digital YA production is influenced by all the networks and modalities they encounter.

Words Traversing Worlds: Two Vignettes

In the section that follows, Rabani presents two vignettes that explore the multimodal artifacts created by her student Shyamu. Significantly, these artifacts traverse modalities, engaging not only with the digital but also with print media, photography, and physical artifacts. Rabani ends this section by presenting several suggestions for how teachers might engage their students in similar work.

1. These youth live at a children's home run by an NGO through the Child Welfare Committee (Government of India). They are deemed to be in need of care and protection by the state.

Vignette 1: RedBubble Scarf

In the summer of 2020, during the height of the Black Lives Matter movement in the United States and an intense period of COVID lockdown in India, Shyamu created a poster inspired by BLM (see Figure 5.1). He painted this picture of an African American woman for an art project at the children's home where he lived at the time. This was not created in response to a prompt on BLM at school or at the home with the volunteers who came to work on art projects. Instead, he explained he had been reading about BLM on Facebook and Instagram through the accounts he follows (friends and influencers) and watching YouTube videos to learn more about the topic. He also mentioned that his teacher had brought it up for a brief discussion at school. A few months later, he put his artwork up on Redbubble, a global online marketplace for print-on-demand products based on user-submitted artwork that gives a certain percentage of the sale amount to the artist. He had seen the site on his social media network. Shyamu's shifts between the digital and the nondigital are inspired by digital YA culture and allow him to create a nondigital multimodal artifact that he then shares digitally. In his example, educators can see the fluidity with which youth move across platforms, networks, and modalities, and the varied ways the digital can, and in fact does, influence nondigital YA production.

Illustrating his knowledge of the ways digital YA production employs multiple digital platforms and modes of communication, Shyamu's writing practice moved multiple spaces including:

- physical space within his community at the home, where he created the art
- digital space, which included mediated sites (social network sites and the website) where he learned about BLM
- geographical boundaries, where he learned about RedBubble
- a global online marketplace, where he displayed his work

FIGURE 5.1. Rabani holding Shyamu's artwork on a scarf she bought on Redbubble.

The creation and circulation of this piece of digital and multimodal writing (i.e., his artwork) emerged through and in conversation with the wider literacy ecosystems Shyamu is a part of. As we see from the above vignette, youth writing in a networked environment is situated within that youth's own local social context but is also in conversation with different platforms connected to digital YA culture. Drawing from the various narratives they encounter, young people carry these connections across virtual and physical geographies and enact their writing practices across different interconnected platforms and spaces.

I, Rabani, encourage teachers to reflect upon how they might leverage students' literacy ecosystems to incorporate varied modalities and digital tools as they work to engage students in meaningful and thought-provoking lessons. In the above example, Shyamu's artwork was made for an informal and out-of-school project, but it was deeply influenced by both local and global digital networks as well as conversations that started *in* school. What might it mean for teachers to challenge students to take what they learn in schools and apply their own literate knowledge as they create multimodal artifacts they can share with their larger digital communities? In the following vignette, teachers will see how narratives from school and information from digitally mediated networks shaped Shyamu's writing project for a formal academic blog.

Vignette 2: Canva as a Multimodal Makerspace

Rabani's students were invited by a youth studies collective in India in the fall of 2020 to contribute to their blog "about moments when they felt compelled to speak about issues that mattered to them" (The Critical Childhood and Youth Studies Collective, personal communication, August 12, 2020). In response to this call, Shyamu made a multimodal piece of artwork entitled "The New Normal." It was a collage of news headlines from 2017 about a Muslim doctor who was wrongly incarcerated by the state for deaths in a hospital in a city in India (IANS, 2019). Shyamu layered these headlines onto a sketch of a large red boot shown stomping a stethoscope that had an emblem of Islam and a heart drawn on it (see Figure 5.2). He shared that his collage drew inspiration from Banksy's works. At school, Shyamu had been introduced to Banksy, a contemporary (anonymous) British street artist and activist who uses his art to target social and political agendas (Artnet, www.artnet.com/artists/banksy/). Shyamu pulled together the news headlines from different digital media networks and sites, including YouTube. A rise in religiously inspired political rhetoric and movements in India in the last few years (Vaishnav, 2019), coupled with the proliferation of highly networked and digitally mediated spaces and technologies of reading and writing, has meant that youth engage and/or encounter digital YAL and connected narratives across multiple media spaces—through media platforms (like Facebook, Instagram, YouTube) and members on it (friends, influencers, celebrities). Rabani's students in India, most of whom are from minority communities, have often shared their discomfort about these discourses that have included a redefinition of national identity. Shyamu's artwork stemmed from these discourses that are a part of his literacy ecosystem.

In this second vignette (see Figure 5.2), teachers can see that the form of Shyamu's writing was shaped by an interconnected literacy ecosystem—one that brought together a school-based writing task with activist artistry heralded across the globe. Moreover, this ecosystem shaped Shyamu's process of creating his piece, and its dissemination traversed multiple modalities, including verbal, pictorial, and more. Significantly, Shyamu's expansive network invited his writing to be political, and like the previous artifact (see Figure 5.1), these politics stemmed from experiences and conversations he was a part of both in and outside of school, online and in person.

Teachers might encourage students to engage in work similar to Shyamu's by introducing them to various digital artists who take up work with themes related to social justice as well as current events related to those themes. Then, they might invite students to respond by creating a piece of artwork and posting it to their school or class blog, allowing them to traverse multiple digital platforms and modalities as Shyamu did. One example of artists engaging in this work—alongside educators—is Bisa Butler, who recently engaged in a virtual talk with Gholdy Muhammad about storytelling through art (https://tinyurl.com/StorytellingThroughArt). Students might watch the video (which was created specifically for a student audience) and then draw upon their own literacies to create a narrative through art and submit it to a class discussion board.

FIGURE 5.2. Shyamu used Canva, an online graphic design platform, to make the poster.

As practitioners who work with young adults, teachers who learn more about the different ways students use, engage, and participate on and through digitally mediated networks can provide important understandings of how to use "appropriate pedagogy" to teach digital YA production in today's digital era (*Preparing Teachers*, 2018). Teachers might look to youth engagement with digital resources and media—specifically understanding how young people design their interactions across multiple modalities, digital platforms, and networks—to expand pedagogical approaches to reading and writing digital YAL and embracing digital YA culture. Rabani offers several suggestions (see sidebar on p. 86) for projects teachers might bring into their classrooms that allow students to critically engage in multimodal and digital writing.

Through the above vignettes, teachers can see that Shyamu's writing, for both formal and informal spaces and projects, is informed by the conversations and networks he is a part of. Youth literacy practices draw upon multiple interconnected spaces and people and traverse multiple contexts. Creating binaries around formal and informal or school and out-of-school literacy practices ignores the ways in which digital YAL reading and writing circulates across networks (Hull & Schultz, 2001). Instead, blurring the lines of what students do both in and out of school allows teachers the opportunity to position students as experts of their own lives and literacies and creates space for even more creative, rich, and rigorous digital YA production.

Projects to Bring to Your Classrooms

Here are a few project ideas that critically engage with youth writing by inviting in conversations from students' literacy ecosystems.

1. **Open-ended writing prompts**: Invite students to write (in any form) about something they have been thinking about, moments they felt compelled to write or do something about, or issues they care about. This can offer a great starting point for a dialogue with student writing.
2. **Tracing ideas**: Ask students to think about the various online and offline influences on the last piece of writing they did. This writing could be a post they wrote or shared, a story they saved or sent to a friend, a picture they took, a TikTok video or reel they made, an essay they wrote. Invite them to share the various spaces they might have engaged with in the process of writing. Online tools like Padlet are great for shared dialogues in classrooms and also offer tools students can use to draw out connections with other students or networks.
3. **A non-text-based response:** Invite students to respond to a question or a prompt using non-text-based modes. Using just memes as a response, making a video, creating an Instagram story, a mini-podcast, and drawings are just a few examples. Your students will have many ideas on how to respond.
4. **Student-designed projects:** Position students as the knowers and the teachers as learners. Creating opportunities for students to be in charge of the learning design for a particular lesson not only brings up new ideas of engagement but also helps shift the power balance a little in the class. This is especially true for projects where teachers are willing participants in the learning.

Things to Keep in Mind

1. Students are used to performing school-based literacy in prescribed ways. Making space for students to bring in their other literacies requires a continuous and conscious effort from teachers. Making it a safe space, focusing on the process, and providing scaffolds to students all help nurture students' literacy practices.
2. Some students might not want to share or be willing to participate in these projects. They might want to keep their school spaces separate. Teachers must acknowledge this and have an alternate option.
3. Coming into the space of youth literacy practices as a learner can offer valuable insights to teachers into how and where their students are reading and writing. Further, youth have a lot of knowledge about new media spaces, and this could be a great opportunity to learn from them.

Conclusion

Today, screens are filled with stories produced by and for young adults. From streaming true crime vlogs on YouTube to watching our friends' vacations unfold on Instagram to scrolling through makeup tutorials and inside jokes on TikTok, youth engagement with digital platforms and devices is often motivated by a desire to engage with others' stories and share their own.

However, these stories—what we understand as one form of digital YAL—that appear across young people's screens are not neutral and neither are the platforms through which they are distributed. The stories that fill screens across the globe often perpetuate dominant cultural and social ideologies. These "dominant narratives, [which originate] from perspectives of groups that hold power and privilege, collectively uphold particular interpretations of reality" (Bacon & Lalvani, 2019, p. 387), and dominant ideologies also perpetuate how narratives are disseminated across online platforms. It is important to recognize these dominant narratives and how they function as the "mainstream narrative[s] in society, which [are] spread through the mass media or other forms of social interaction, resulting in stigmatization and opportunity deprivation" (Zhang, 2019). For this reason, and as articulated above, ELA teachers have a responsibility not only to teach their students how to critically engage with and create written narratives within their classrooms but also to guide students in critiquing the dominant narratives they encounter online. Moreover, teachers might provide students with opportunities and tools to critically and creatively restory those dominant narratives through digital YA production. In the examples above, students were presented with dominant narratives about going to college and Black Lives Matter and used digital tools to restory those narratives and position themselves as experts and knowledge producers in the process. To guide students in this work, teachers themselves need to become educated in how these digital dominant narratives impact students and consider how "appropriate pedagogy" might shift to embrace "freedom and autonomy" (*Preparing Teachers*, 2018) in students' production of digital YAL. Engaging with students in the critique and creation of digital YA cultural narratives, including digital YAL, will provide teachers a more holistic look as to why it's important for students to recognize, resist, and restory dominant narratives on digital platforms, from Wattpad stories to YouTube videos.

Thus, composing digital YAL by engaging digital YA culture and creating digital YA artifacts is ripe with opportunities for teachers to restory both ELA curricula and pedagogy alongside students, creating opportunities for them to take the lead as they engage their out-of-school literacy practices in classrooms. Further, engaging students in the act of digital YA composing allows students to restory their own narratives, especially those that are deficit-based and written about them from majoritarian perspectives that do not value their lives, experiences, or knowledges. The stories presented above are written by students alongside educators who care for them deeply and recognize their brilliance and all they have to offer the world. As such, engaging digital YA storytelling in the classroom—much like un-whitewashing curricula (see chapter four)—is a practice that is not only a useful practice to take up in ELA classrooms, but also one that recognizes and affirms the humanity of all students, making it a useful practice for all who engage in literacy learning with students. In our final chapter, "Restorying the Future toward Hope," we (Josh, Autumn, and Ebony) explore the potential of restorying young adult literature for futures to come, and we do so in pursuit of hope-filled futures that challenge "damage" narratives (Tuck, 2009) around historically marginalized communities in English language arts.

Restorying the Future toward Hope: A Conclusion

Chapter Six

Throughout this book, we the primary authors have, with support from our contributing authors, articulated the means by which adolescents, teachers, librarians, and researchers restory various aspects of literacy learning in English classrooms (i.e., text selection, digital access, YAL curriculum, and multimodality), and we have done so to account for the rapid pace at which technology is evolving. We argue that accounting for such change not only prepares students for today's digital era but also provides them agency and choice over how to practice their varied literacies and to engage with texts in the world around them. Further, it invites students and their literacies into the conversation rather than casting them further away from their own learning by centering deficit perspectives. In *Restorying Young Adult Literature*, we have demonstrated how teachers might effectively, as Eve Tuck (2009) eloquently articulates, "suspend damage," doing so while also turning our attention toward more hope-filled futures for all learners.

As we bring this book to a close, in this chapter, we focus on two major takeaways we hope English educators will find useful as they reflect upon how to integrate digital YAL and digital YA culture into their work with adolescents:

1. In today's digital age, young adult literature itself has changed, forming digital YAL with unique textual affordances.
2. Also, in today's digital age, YAL is nestled in a participatory network that forms a digital YA culture.

We use these takeaways to synthesize the major themes of the book, making connections across chapters, authors, and topics. We then conclude this chapter and this book by turning our attention toward what we believe to be the hopeful—and restoried—futures that are possible when we engage digital YAL in thoughtful and meaningful ways as English educators.

Takeaway 1: In Today's Digital Age, YAL Itself Has Changed

As referenced both in our introduction and in chapter two, texts no longer hold the nostalgia of yesteryear. As both our society and technology rapidly grow and change, so, too, do young adult literature texts. Ranging from digital YAL to blogs, social media feeds, and podcasts, educators and adolescents have a myriad of resources from which they can select texts and an equally long list of platforms from which they can engage these texts through critical pedagogy. In chapter two, "Restorying Text Selection," we acknowledge that all of these choices can feel overwhelming for teachers, and we demonstrate how restorying text selection might serve as a guide for teachers as they work toward becoming critical, antiracist, trans- and queer-affirming pedagogues.

One way teachers can actively restory text selection and engage with YAL in this digital age is by "know[ing] the literature." As mentioned in both chapters two and four, #DisruptTexts, created by four women of color, provides teachers with more inclusive and restorative options for text selection, both physical and digital. The #DisruptTexts platform itself is a website with recommended readings, a statement, curriculum suggestions, and archived Twitter chats amongst participating teachers. By familiarizing themselves with platforms like #DisruptTexts, teachers not only come to "know the [young adult] literature" (e.g., digital YAL) but also to become experts on the discourse and platforms available through digital YA culture. By restorying their text selection, educators might broaden their teacher networks as they engage the digital.

Additionally, as texts, platforms, and technology continually shift, the modes through which students—and thus teachers—engage digital YAL and digital YA culture change as well. As noted in the *Preparing Teachers with Knowledge of Children's and Young Adult Literature* position statement (2018), "teaching children's and young adult literature is about more than getting students to fall in love with reading," but that "teachers also need to know evidence-based strategies for supporting student knowledge of literary crafting." In chapters four and five, we spoke at length about how a focus on multimodality in adolescent English education helps students to develop a knowledge of how to craft their own stories, questions, and critical analyses of the world around them. Restorying multimodality for a twenty-first-century context is one way teachers can employ "appropriate pedagogy" (Buehler et al., 2018) to include students' own funds of knowledge (Moll et al., 1992) in ELA classrooms. Furthermore, educators can help their students consider how their work online might translate to physical contexts and thus engage social networks with an expansive audience of readers. When students understand the affordances of the multimodal and how it allows them to traverse worlds, they are able to critically engage the world around them, and teachers need only provide space for students to exercise "freedom and autonomy" in the production of digital YAL (*Preparing Teachers*, 2018).

Takeaway 2: In Today's Digital Age, YAL Is Nestled in Networked Culture

As defined in chapter one, digital YA culture refers to varied digital platforms that allow young adults and YA enthusiasts to disseminate, discuss, and engage with YAL and media. We explain that YA culture is participatory and, borrowing from Jenkins (2006), characterize it as having:

1. Relatively low barriers to artistic expression and civic engagement,
2. Strong support for creating and sharing one's creations with others,
3. Some type of informal mentorship whereby what is known by the most experienced is passed along to the novices,
4. Belief from members that their contributions matter, and
5. Feeling some degree of social connection among members (at the least, they care what other people think about what they have created).

In acknowledging and taking up these characteristics, English educators work toward effectively restorying YA culture alongside youth, leveraging the affordances of the digital and centering the knowledges, experiences, and lives of young adults in recognizing the pedagogical affordances of digital YA culture.

School and community librarians and media specialists bring a unique set of skills and knowledges to the table in this regard. As noted in chapter three, "Restorying Digital Access," these literacy professionals are readers who not only live literate lives themselves (*Preparing Teachers*, 2018) but have knowledge and often training not afforded to English educators in teacher preparation programs. Thus, they serve as deep wells of knowledge in assisting teachers in navigating digital resources and facilitating opportunities for students to engage in and continue to build upon digital YA culture. As such, it is imperative that teachers "invest in relationships with librarians" (*Preparing Teachers*, 2018). So, we implore teachers not only to learn from the excerpts included from librarians in chapter three but to reach out to their school and community librarians for support in curating these resources for their classrooms.

In addition to librarians, teachers can learn with and from their students and the ways they already engage with various digital platforms and digital networks. In doing so, English educators leverage students' access to and understanding of digital YAL and digital YA culture in their classrooms as they create learning environments and experiences that honor, center, and uplift students' knowledges, positioning them as experts in their own right. In chapter four, "Restorying YAL Curricula," we addressed the specific ways English educators can integrate technology and all of its affordances to restory and un-whitewash curricula as they work alongside students and learn from the varied communities in which they already participate. We noted how working alongside students and engaging fan communities in the classrooms not only affirms diversity but also facilitates opportunities for students—and teachers—to exercise critical literacy in their classrooms. As educators prepare students for a world beyond the walls of the classroom, teaching students to enact their critical literacies and draw upon their own skills and knowledges is crucial.

Imagining Future Worlds and English Classrooms

Just for a moment, imagine with us a world thirty years from now. The students who currently take up space in our classrooms are now adults. Some may have classrooms of their own. Others may be leaders of organizations, cities, or states. Others may be parents, construction workers, bloggers, hairstylists, or inhabiting a myriad of other futures they've crafted for themselves. As we, authors and readers together, think about these futures, imagine how our classrooms prepared them for their roles. Did we teach them to critically think for themselves so they could find causes important to them, or did we teach them to regurgitate information? Did we leverage the digital tools they use in their everyday lives to teach them to acquire the skills they desire for their futures, or did we stifle learning with inauthentic digital experiences (Griffin, 2021)? Did we present texts that provided them not only with windows, mirrors, and sliding glass doors but also with telescopes (Toliver, 2021) that made "faraway, liberatory ideas clearer and brighter" (p. 30)? How did we present opportunities for students to create content and tell their own stories? To learn from literacy experts with knowledge different from our own? What role did we play? Further, how did the education we provided, the lessons we taught, and the tools we engaged impact our own lives in this not-too-distant future?

The lives our students lead in the future are partly determined by how and what we teach today. As professionals who have chosen education as our work, we have to understand that "education is an investment in other people's lives and communities" as much as it is "an investment in our [own] lives" (Kinloch, 2022, p. 34). We are at a time when educators are uniquely positioned to leverage digital resources to transform and restory English education forever. And quite frankly, whether we make the choice or not, the digital will continue to change, shift, morph, and develop. It is our hope that this book serves as a resource for teachers looking to restory English education by creating more justice-centered, liberated, decolonized, and antiracist futures alongside students, librarians, and digital teacher communities. We hope this book helps you to restory English education's exclusionary past. Moreover, we hope it provides you pedagogical approaches for crafting a more just future for English language arts—one in which those students who have been pushed farthest to the margins instead read, write, and imagine from the center of our classrooms, communities, and world.

Annotated Bibliography

Critical YAL Readings

Garcia, A. (2013). *Critical foundations in young adult literature: Challenging genres.* Sense Publishers.

This book foregrounds historical approaches to the study of YAL from a critical perspective. It's a useful primer for teachers and students as it lays out YAL's role in realizing social justice. Teachers can use this text to familiarize themselves with critical literacy-based approaches to YAL.

Thomas, E. E. (2019). *The dark fantastic: Race and the imagination from Harry Potter to the Hunger Games.* New York University Press.

Exploring the placement of race in speculative YAL and media, this book reveals how the diversity crisis in YA literature and media stems from an imagination gap. Teachers can use it to explore the development of their own and students' imaginations relative to diverse representation.

Thomas, E. E., & Stornaiuolo, A. (2016). Restorying the self: Bending toward textual justice. *Harvard Educational Review, 86*(3), 313–338. https://doi.org/10.17763/1943-5045-86.3.313

This article reveals the foundations of restorying as a concept that can be used in ELA classrooms. It also provides teachers with inroads for welcoming fan studies into classrooms and for teaching restorying through literary study.

Platforms

Canva
www.canva.com/

User-friendly platform that supports the online graphic design of social media posts, presentations, posters, videos, and more. Teachers might use this platform to create anchor charts, presentations, and other pedagogical tools.

Flip, formerly Flipgrid
info.flip.com/

Free online platform for creating and sequencing video discussions within a classroom. This tool can support students in building classroom culture and crafting robust literary discussion through digital technology.

Padlet
padlet.com/

Online cloud-based platform that allows students to share content around a given topic. The interface takes place on virtual bulletin boards set up by the teacher. Padlet allows students to organize and share digital resources connected to studies of literary representation.

Redbubble
www.redbubble.com/

Online marketplace for sharing artwork across the globe. This space allows students to interact and to share their creations with the world, and it can be used to support students in their digital YA production.

TikTok
www.tiktok.com/

Social media platform where teachers and students share video content and connect with communities across the globe. This platform can be used to learn about digital YA as well as to connect with other teachers and students interested in diversity in YAL.

Twitter
twitter.com/

Social media platform where teachers and students share short written texts, news articles, and short videos with audiences across the globe. This platform can be used to share links and create networks and participatory communities around digital YAL.

YouTube
www.youtube.com/

Video hosting platform where students and teachers can share original content. This resource can provide supplementary resources for teaching digital YAL as well as free audiobooks on occasion.

Wattpad
www.wattpad.com/

Online repository for fanfiction that provides inline annotation features, commenting functions, and liking buttons to bring readers and writers into conversation. This platform can be a nice introduction for students to engage in fan writing and build community around digital YAL.

Blogs

We Need Diverse Books
diversebooks.org/

Resource for advocacy efforts around locating and teaching diverse books. Teachers can use this website to locate diverse digital YAL for their classrooms.

Build Your Stack
ncte.org/build-your-stack/

NCTE (National Council of Teachers of English) resource share to support teachers expanding their knowledge of diverse books. This website provides strategies and community through which teachers can expand their knowledge of digital YAL and diversity.

Booktoss
booktoss.org/

Blog by Laura Jiménez that encourages tossing books that are problematic. This website provides criticism on contemporary digital YAL that teachers might bring to their classrooms.

The Conscious Kid
www.theconsciouskid.org/

Education blog focused on healthy racial identity development. This website provides resources like read-alouds and booklist recommendations for teachers.

Reading While White
readingwhilewhite.blogspot.com/

Blog by white librarians to support white readers in embracing diverse books. This website provides criticism about whiteness and anti-Blackness in digital YAL and can support white teachers in developing racial literacies.

Lee and Low
blog.leeandlow.com/

Publisher blog that explores race and other forms of diversity in education. This open blog curates criticism and recommendations of teachable YAL. Tags across blog posts can support teachers in crafting robust curricula and diversifying their text selection.

Reading Spark
readingspark.wordpress.com/

Blog by Sarah Dahlen that focuses on Asian/Asian American representation. This resource specifically focuses on adoption and the Korean diaspora and can be used to locate diverse YAL to inform curricula.

Disability in Kid Lit
disabilityinkidlit.com/

Blog focused on disabilities representation. Though now defunct, this blog houses historical criticism of disability representation and an "honor roll" of notable YAL featuring disabled characters that teachers might use to inform their text selection.

YA Pride
www.ya-pride.org/

Blog focused on LGBTQIA+ representation in young adult literature. This blog provides an easily searchable "master list" of LGBTQIA+ representation in digital YAL that can inform teachers' text selection.

Latinx in Kid Lit
latinosinkidlit.com/

Blog focused on Latinx representation in kid lit. This blog provides book reviews of Latinx YAL as well as lists of resources and illustrator spotlights that might inform pedagogy around Latinx YAL.

Digital YAL Initiatives

#ReadWoke

This hashtag supports locating Read Woke books. This was started by award-winning librarian Cecily Lewis and is intended to amplify voices of BIPOC and other disenfranchised communities.

#DisruptTexts

This is a grassroots, teacher-led initiative that seeks to push against the canon in ELA by foregrounding more inclusive, representative, and equitable representation.

#OwnVoices

Begun by YA author Corinne Duyvis, #OwnVoices is a hashtag used to spotlight texts in which the author's lived experiences reflect the lived experiences of the main character.

#WeNeedDiverseBooks

This hashtag is based on the nonprofit organization of the same name. This movement seeks to support ELA educators in locating intersectional, diverse texts and text sets based on the needs of your classroom.

Works Cited

AASL. (2009). *Standards for the 21st-century learner in action*. American Association of School Librarians.

Adichie, C. N. (2009). *The danger of a single story* [Video]. TED Conferences. https://www.ted.com/talks/chimamanda_adichie_the_danger_of_a_single_story

Ahlfeld, K. (2019). They paved paradise: School librarians and school libraries are disappearing and we won't know what we've lost until it's gone. *Journal of Library Administration*, *59*(8), 927–938.

Anderson, M., & Jiang, J. (2018, May 31). *Teens, social media & technology*. Pew Research Center. https://www.pewresearch.org/internet/2018/05/31/teens-social-media-technology-2018/

Appleman, D. (2015). *Critical encounters in secondary English: Teaching literary theory to adolescents*. Teachers College Press.

Bacon, J. K., & Lalvani, P. (2019). Dominant narratives, subjugated knowledges, and the righting of the story of disability in K–12 curricula. *Curriculum Inquiry, 49*(4), 387–404.

Baker-Bell, A., Butler, T., & Johnson, L. (2017). The pain and the wounds: A call for critical race English education in the wake of racial violence. *English Education, 49*(2), 116–129.

Bamberger, C., Bryan, C., Campbell, J., & Schultz, A. (2020, July 1). As COVID-19 budget cuts loom, relevance of school librarians put to the test. *Education Week*. Retrieved March 9, 2021, from https://www.edweek.org/teaching-learning/as-covid-19-budget-cuts-loomrelevance-of-school-librarians-put-to-the-test/2020/07

Benbow, C. (2016). *Lemonade syllabus*. Texas A&M University Office for Diversity. https://diversity.tamu.edu/Diversity/media/diversity/PDF/lemonade-syllabus.pdf

Beyoncé, & Joseph, K. (Directors). (2016). *Lemonade* [Film]. Parkwood Entertainment.

Bishop, R. (1990). Mirrors, windows, and sliding glass doors. *Perspectives, 6*(3), ix–xi.

Borsheim-Black, C., & Sarigianides, S. T. (2019). *Letting go of literary whiteness: Antiracist literature instruction for white students*. Teachers College Press.

Braun, L. W., Hartman, M. L., Hughes-Hassell, S., & Kumasi, K. (2014). *The future of library services for and with teens: A call to action*. YALSA. http://www.ala.org/yaforum/sites/ala.org.yaforum/files/content/YALSA_nationalforum_F inal_web_0.pdf

Buehler, J., Dávila, D., McClure, A., & Miller, D. (2018). *Preparing teachers with knowledge of children's and young adult literature*. National Council of Teachers of English. Retrieved January 17, 2022, from https://ncte.org/statement/chiladollitguideline/print/

Campbell, E. (2010, September 26). About me. *Cotton Quilts*. https://crazyquiltedi.blog/me-2-0/

Carlton, A. (2016, September 8). *Speaking out against Chicago school library cuts*. American Libraries. https://americanlibrariesmagazine.org/blogs/the-scoop/speaking-out-against-chicago-school-library-cuts/

Cart, M. (2016). Young adult literature: The state of a restless art. *SLIS Connecting, 5*(1). https://doi.org/10.18785/slis.0501.07

CCBC. (2020). Books by and/or about black, indigenous and people of color (all years). Cooperative Children's Book Center. https://ccbc.education.wisc.edu/literature-resources/ccbc-diversity-statistics/books-by-about-poc-fnn/

Chouliaraki, L. (2015). Digital witnessing in conflict zones: The politics of remediation. *Information, Communication & Society*, *18*(11), 1362–1377. https://doi.org/10.1080/1369118X.2015.1070890

Coleman, J. J. (2019). Digital innocence: Queer

virginity, painful histories, and the critical hope of queer futurity. *Research on Diversity in Youth Literature, 2*(1), 1–19.

Coleman, J. J., & Hall, L. (2019). What story, what identity, Wattpad: Teaching youth to restory YA literature. *The ALAN Review*, Winter, 65–70.

Coleman, J. J. (2020). *Restorying painful histories: Critical literacy, the imagination gap, and the affective lives of queer educators* (Publication No. 3851) [Doctoral dissertation, University of Pennsylvania]. Scholarly Commons dissertations and thesis database. https://repository.upenn.edu/edissertations/3851

Coleman, J. J. (2021). Affective reader response: using ordinary affects to repair literacy normativities in ELA and english education. *English Education*, 23.

Coleman, J. J. (2022). The fabulous rhetorics of queer inhumanity: Speculating with queer inhuman figures to restory queerphobic histories. In J. Rhodes & J. Alexander (Eds.), *The Routledge handbook of queer rhetoric*. Routledge.

Connelly, F. M., & Clandinin, D. J. (2006). Narrative inquiry. In J. L. Green, G. Camilli, P. B. Elmore, & E. Grace (Eds.), *Handbook of complementary methods in education research*. Lawrence Erlbaum.

Coogler, R. (Director). (2018). *Black Panther* [Film]. Marvel Studios/Walt Disney Pictures.

Cooper, M. (2017). *Family values: Between neoliberalism and the new social conservatism*. Zone Books.

Crenshaw, K. (1991). Mapping the margins: Intersectionality, identity politics, and violence against women of color. *Stanford Law Review, 43*(6), 1241–1299.

Dahlen, S. P., & Thomas, E. E. (Eds.). (2022). *Harry Potter and the other: Race, justice, and difference in the* wizarding *world*. University Press of Mississippi.

Daiute, C., & Lightfoot, C. (Eds.). (2004). *Narrative analysis: Studying the development of individuals in society*. Sage.

de los Ríos, C. V., Martinez, D. C., Musser, A. D., Canady, A., Camangian, P., & Quijada, P. D. (2019). Upending colonial practices: Toward repairing harm in English education. *Theory into Practice, 58*(4), 359–367. https://doi.org/10.1080/00405841.2019.1626615

DiMartino, M. D., Ehasz, A., & Konietzko, B. (Executive Producers). (2005–2008). *Avatar: The last airbender* [TV series]. Nickelodeon.

Ebarvia, T. (2021, January 2). *January 2021 statement*. #DisruptTexts. https://disrupttexts.org/2021/01/02/january-2021-statement/

Ebarvia, T., Germán, L., Parker, K. N., & Torres, J. (2020). #DisruptTexts: An introduction. *English Journal, 110*(1), 100–102.

Ellison, T. L., & Solomon, M. (2019). Counter-storytelling vs. deficit thinking around African American children and families, digital literacies, race, and the digital divide. *Research in the Teaching of English, 53*(3), 223–244.

Fitzgerald, F. S. (1925). *The great Gatsby*. Charles Scribner's Sons.

Freire, P. (1970). *Pedagogy of the oppressed*. Herder and Herder.

Freire, P., & Macedo, D. (2005). *Literacy: Reading the word and the world*. London: Routledge.

Gardner, M. E. (2020). School librarians are collaboration superheroes: This issue of *Knowledge Quest* explores ways that our fellow superhero school librarians are forming powerful collaborative relationships. *Knowledge Quest, 49*(2), 6–7.

Gonzalez, M., & SG, M. (2022). Children's books as a radical act. *Reflection Press*. https://reflectionpress.com/childrens-books-radicalact/

Good, T. (2013, February 6). Manufacturing makerspaces: Three makerspace models that work. American Libraries. https://americanlibrariesmagazine.org/2013/02/06/manufacturing-makerspaces/

Graham, K. A. (2020, January 24). Philly's got the worst school librarian ratio in the U.S. This group is protesting. *The Philadelphia Inquirer*. https://www.inquirer.com/education/school-library-librarians-closed-philadelphia-rally-ratio-20200124.html

Greason, W. (2016, June 19). Introduction to the #Wakandasyllabus. *Black Perspectives.* https://www.aaihs.org/introduction-to-the-wakanda-syllabus/.

Green, P. (2018). Teacher librarians are your literacy partners. *The Reading Teacher, 72*(3), 404. https://doi-org.proxy.library.upenn.edu/10.1002/trtr.1727

Gretes, F. (2013). *School library impact studies: A review of findings and guide to sources.* Harry & Jeanette Weinberg Foundation.

Griffin, A., & James, A. (2018). Humanities curricula as white property: Toward a reclamation of black creative thought in social studies & literacy curricula. *Multicultural Education, 25*(3), 10–17.

Griffin, A. A. (2021). A digital mismatch: Adolescent black girls' perceptions of the usefulness of digital tools. In D. Price-Dennis & G. E. Muhammad (Eds.), *Black girls' literacies: Transforming lives and literacy practices* (pp. 218–238). Routledge.

Griffin, A. A., & Turner, J. D. (2021). Toward a pedagogy of black livingness: Black students' creative multimodal renderings of resistance to anti-blackness. *English Teaching: Practice & Critique, 20*(4), 440-453.

The Guardian. (2019, April 8). *Eight black women discuss the politics of skin tone* [Video]. YouTube. https://www.youtube.com/watch?v=i3rEZnxOWcw

Haddix, M., & Sealey-Ruiz, Y. (2012). Cultivating digital and popular literacies as empowering and emancipatory acts among urban youth. *Journal of Adolescent & Adult Literacy, 56*(3), 189–192.

Harris, C. I. (1993). Whiteness as property. *Harvard Law Review, 106*(8), 1707–1791.

Hughes, H. (2014). School libraries, teacher-librarians and student outcomes: Presenting and using the evidence. *School Libraries Worldwide, 20*(1), 29–50.

Hull, G., & Schultz, K. (2001). Literacy and learning out of school: A review of theory and research. *Review of Educational Research, 71*(4), 575–611. https://doi.org/10.3102/00346543071004575

Huyck, D., & Dahlen, S. P. (2019, June 19). Diversity in children's books 2018. *sarahpark.com* blog. Created in consultation with Edith Campbell, Molly Beth Griffin, K. T. Horning, Debbie Reese, Ebony Elizabeth Thomas, and Madeline Tyner, with statistics compiled by the Cooperative Children's Book Center, School of Education, University of Wisconsin-Madison. https://ccbc.education.wisc.edu/literature-resources/ccbc-diversity-statistics/books-by-about-poc-fnn/. Retrieved from https://readingspark.wordpress.com/2019/06/19/picture-this-diversity-in-childrens-books-2018-infographic/.

IANS. (2019). Gorakhpur hospital tragedy: Dr. Kafeel Khan seeks apology from Yogi Adityanath government. *The New Indian Express.* https://www.newindianexpress.com/nation/2019/oct/01/gorakhpur-hospital-tragedy-dr-kafeel-khan-seeks-apology-from-yogi-adityanath-government-2041721.html

Inklebarger, T. (2019, November 8). How the CPS strike affected Chicago school librarians. *American Libraries.* https://americanlibrariesmagazine.org/2019/11/08/cps-strike-affected-chicago-school-librarians/

Ishizuka, K., & Stephens, R. (2019). The cat is out of the bag: Orientalism, anti-blackness, and white supremacy in Dr. Seuss's children's books. *Research on Diversity in Youth Literature, 1*(2).

Jenkins, H. (2006). *Confronting the challenges of participatory culture: Media education for the 21st Century.* MIT Press.

Jenkins, H. (2013). *Textual poachers: Television fans and participatory culture.* Routledge.

Jenkins, H., Ito, M., & boyd, danah. (2016). *Participatory culture in a networked era.* Polity Press.

Johnson, L. L., Gibbs Grey, T. D., & Baker-Bell, A. (2017). Changing the dominant narrative: A call for using storytelling as language and literacy theory, research methodology, and practice. *Journal of Literacy Research, 49*(4), 467–475.

Johnson, L. P. (2017). Writing the self: Black queer youth challenge heteronormative ways of being in an after-school writing club. *Research in the Teaching of English, 52*(1), 13–33.

Kapitzke, C. (2001). Information literacy: The changing library. *Journal of Adolescent & Adult Literacy, 44*(5), 450–456.

Kelly, L. L. (2018). A Snapchat story: How black girls develop strategies for critical resistance in school. *Learning, Media and Technology, 43*(4), 374–389.

Kinloch, V. (2022). Education as freedom/education is freedom. *Council Chronicle, 31*(3), 34.

Lance, K.C., & Kachel, D. E. (2018, March 26). Why school librarians matter: What years of research tell us. *Phi Delta Kappan*. https://kappanonline.org/lance-kachel-school-librarians-matter-years-research/

Larrick, N. (1965). The all-white world of children's books. *Saturday Review*, 62–65 and 85.

Lee, H. (1960). *To kill a mockingbird.* J. B. Lippincott & Co.

Lee, S. (1988). *School daze* [Film]. 40 Acres and a Mule Filmworks.

Lewis, C. (2017, November 20). #ReadWoke. *Cicelythegreat*. https://cicelythegreat.wordpress.com/2017/11/20/readwoke/

Lewis, C. (2019, February 26). Read woke across America week. *Cicelythegreat.* https://cicelythegreat.wordpress.com/2019/02/26/read-woke-across-america-week/

Love, B. (2019). *We want to do more than survive: Abolitionist teaching and the pursuit of educational freedom*. Beacon Press.

McLemore, A. M. (2018). Roja. In S. Mitchell (Ed.), *All out: The no-longer-secret stories of queer teens throughout the ages*. Harlequin Teen.

Messina, C. M. (2019). Tracing fan uptakes: Tagging, language, and ideological practices in *The Legend of Korra* fanfictions. *The Journal of Writing Analytics, 3*, 151–182.

Mirra, N., & Garcia, A. (2020). "I hesitate but I do have hope": Youth speculative civic literacies for troubled times. *Harvard Educational Review, 90*(2), 295–321. https://doi.org/10.17763/1943-5045-90.2.295

Moll, L., Amanti, C., Neffe, D., & Gonzále, N. (1992). Funds of knowledge for teaching: Using a qualitative approach to connect homes and classrooms. *Theory Into Practice, 31*(2), 132–141.

Moll, L. C. (2019). Elaborating funds of knowledge: Community-oriented practices in international contexts. *Literacy Research: Theory, Method, and Practice, 68*(1), 130–138.

Moorefield-Lang, H. (2015) Change in the making: Makerspaces and the ever-changing landscape of libraries. *TechTrends 59*(3), 107–112.

Muhammad, G. (2020). *Cultivating genius: An equity framework for culturally and historically responsive literacy*. Scholastic Incorporated.

Muñoz, J. E. (2009). *Cruising Utopia: The then and there of queer futurity*. New York University Press.

National Council of Teachers of English. (2021). *Report of the task force on critical media literacy*. Canva. Retrieved June 27, 2021, from https://www.canva.com/design/DAERz0BpJyk/I4sPUxfrZlHLVys3QIVilQ/view

Nel, P. (2017). *Was the cat in the hat black? The hidden racism of children's literature, and the need for diverse books*. Oxford University Press.

Noble, S. U. (2018). *Algorithms of oppression: How search engines reinforce racism*. New York University Press.

Ollerenshaw, J. A., & Creswell, J. W. (2002). Narrative research: A comparison of two restorying data analysis approaches. *Qualitative Inquiry, 8*(3), 329–347.

Papailias, P. (2016). Witnessing in the age of the database: Viral memorials, affective publics, and the assemblage of mourning. *Memory Studies, 9*(4), 437–454. https://doi.org/10.1177/1750698015622058

Perillo, J. (2017, May 19). *Real teaching in a time of fake news*. National Council of Teachers of English. https://ncte.org/blog/2017/05/real-teaching-time-fake-news/

Potter, N. (2016, November 3). *For the last time, Google is not our competition in libraries.... Ned Potter.* https://www.ned-potter.com/blog/for-the-last-time-google-is-not-our-competition-in-libraries

Price-Dennis, D., & Sealey-Ruiz, Y. (2021). *Advancing racial literacies in teacher education: Activism for equity in digital spaces.* Teachers College Press.

Reese, D., & Mendoza, J. (2022). *About AICL.* American Indians in Children's Literature (AICL). https://americanindiansinchildrensliterature.blogspot.com/p/about.html

Reich, J., & Ito, M. (2017). *From good intentions to real outcomes: Equity by design in learning technologies.* Digital Media + Learning Research Hub. https://clalliance.org/wp-content/uploads/2017/11/GIROreport_1031.pdf

Romano, A. (2016, June 7). *Canon, fanon, shipping and more: A glossary of the tricky terminology that makes up fan culture.* Vox. https://www.vox.com/2016/6/7/11858680/fandom-glossary-fanfiction-explained

Rosenblatt, L. (1995). *Literature as exploration* (5th ed.). Modern Language Association of America.

Rowsell, J., Morrell, E., & Alvermann, D. E. (2017). Confronting the digital divide: Debunking brave new world discourses. *The Reading Teacher, 71*(2), 157–165. https://doi.org/10.1002/trtr.1603

Schey, R. (2017). Toward intersectional literacy practices: Interrogating homonormativity through reading Sáenz's *Aristotle and Dante. The ALAN Review, 45*(1), 32–43.

Slatter, D., & Howard, Z. (2013). A place to make, hack, and learn: Makerspaces in Australian public libraries. *The Australian Library Journal, 62*(4), 272–284. https://doi.org/10.1080/00049670.2013.853335

Stornaiuolo, A., & Thomas, E. E. (2017). Disrupting educational inequalities through youth digital activism. *Review of Research in Education, 41*(1), 337-357.

Stornaiuolo, A., & Thomas, E. E. (2018). Restorying as political action: Authoring resistance through youth media arts. *Learning, Media and Technology, 43*(4), 345-358.

Thomas, E. E. (2019). *The dark fantastic: Race and the imagination from Harry Potter to the Hunger Games.* New York University Press.

Thomas, E. E., & Stornaiuolo, A. (2016). Restorying the self: Bending toward textual justice. *Harvard Educational Review, 86*(3), 313–338. https://doi.org/10.17763/1943-5045-86.3.313

Thomas, E. E., & Stornaiuolo, A. (2019). Race, storying, and restoring: What can we learn from black fans? *Journal of Transformative Works and Cultures 29.* https://journal.transformativeworks.org/index.php/twc/article/view/1562

Toliver, S. (2021). On mirrors, windows, and telescopes. *Council Chronicle, 31*(1), 29–30.

Toliver, S. R., & Hadley, H. L. (2021). Ca(n)non fodder no more: Disrupting common arguments that support a canonical empire. *Journal of Language & Literacy Education, 17*(2), 1–28.

Tuck, E. (2009). Suspending damage: A letter to communities. *Harvard Educational Review, 79*(3), 409–428.

Vaishnav, M. (2019, April 4). *Religious nationalism and India's future.* Carnegie Endowment for International Peace. https://carnegieendowment.org/2019/04/04/religious-nationalism-and-india-s-future-pub-78703

Valenza, J. (2020, November 1). Enough with the CRAAP: We're just not doing it right. *School Library Journal.* https://blogs.slj.com/neverendingsearch/2020/11/01/enough-with-the-craap-were-just-not-doing-it-right/

Wargo, J. M. (2018). #SoundingOutMySilence: Reading a LGBTQ youth's sonic cartography as multimodal (counter)storytelling. *Journal of Adolescent & Adult Literacy, 62*(1), 13–23. https://doi.org/10.1002/jaal.752

Wine, L. D. (2016). School librarians as technology leaders: An evolution in practice. *Journal of Education for Library and Information Science, 57*(2), 207–220.

Wineburg, S., Breakstone, J., Ziv, N., & Smith, M. (2020). *Educating for misunderstanding: How approaches to teaching digital literacy make students susceptible to scammers, rogues, bad actors, and hate mongers* (Working Paper No. A-21322). Stanford History Education Group, Stanford University. https://purl.stanford.edu/mf412bt5333

Witte, S., Bass, B., O'Byrne, W. I., Price-Dennis, D., & Sibberson, F. (2019). *Definition of literacy in a digital age.* National Council of Teachers of English. https://ncte.org/statement/nctes-definition-literacy-digital-age/

Witteveen, A. (2020, November 2). Ahead of the curve: School librarians innovate and take on new responsibilities. *School Library Journal.* https://www.slj.com/?detailStory=ahead-of-the-curve-school-librarians-innovate-take-on-new-responsibilities-SLJ-covid-19-survey

Zhang, L. (2019). Resistance to dominant narratives and the construction of identity legitimacy: Counterstories of Chinese migrant workers with pneumoconiosis. *Chinese Journal of Communication, 12*(2), 147–165. https://doi.org/10.1080/17544750.2018.1511608

Index

The letter *f* following a page locator denotes a figure.

Authors

James Joshua (Josh) Coleman is an assistant professor of English education at the University of Iowa. A former high school teacher, his research interests seek to integrate queer and trans studies scholarship within English education. A member of NCTE since 2015, he is currently a member of the Gender and Sexuality Equity Assembly. His most recent scholarship can be found in *The ALAN Review, Research on Diversity in Youth Literature, English Education,* and *Teaching and Teacher Education.* Please feel free to contact Josh at josh-coleman@uiowa.edu or on Twitter at @JoshEducating.

Autumn A. Griffin is a researcher of Black girlhoods, digital and multimodal literacies, and children's and young adult literature. Having previously taught secondary English language arts in Atlanta, Georgia, her research explores how Black youth use literacies to heal from pedagogical and curricular violence. Autumn's work has been published in the *Journal of Language and Literacy Education, English Teaching: Practice & Critique, Urban Education, Research in the Teaching of English, Language Arts,* and *Multicultural Education.* She is currently working on her second book. Autumn is also a 200-hour registered yoga teacher, and in her spare time, she teaches yoga and enjoys fusing it with Black feminist practices of healing to create sacred spaces for communities of Black folks.

Ebony Elizabeth Thomas, is an associate professor and co-chair of the Joint Program in English and Education at the University of Michigan's School of Education. A notable expert on diversity in children's and young adult literature, she is the award-winning author of *The Dark Fantastic: Race and the Imagination from Harry Potter to the Hunger Games* (2019). Her most recent book is *Harry Potter and the Other: Race, Justice, and Difference in the Wizarding World* (2022), coedited with Sarah Park Dahlen.

This book was typeset in Adobe Caslon Pro and PT Serif by Barbara Frazier.

Typefaces used on the cover include Chronicle Display, Avenir Book, Avenir Next Medium, and Avenir LT Com 65 Medium.

The book was printed on 50-lb. white, offset paper.